THE GOD
of
MIRACLES

MICHAEL H. BROWN

Queenship

PUBLISHING COMPANY
P.O. Box 220 • Goleta, CA 93116
(800) 647-9882 • (805) 692-0043 • Fax: (805) 967-5133
www.queenship.org

Library of Congress Number # 2005909925

Published by:
    Queenship Publishing
    P.O. Box 220
    Goleta, CA 93116
    (800) 647-9882 • (805) 692-0043 • Fax: (805) 967-5133
    www.queenship.org

Printed in the United States of America

ISBN: 1-57918-294-1

For Lisa

Because he hath set his love upon Me, therefore will I deliver him; I will set him on high, because he hath known My Name. He shall call upon Me, and I will answer him: I will be with him in trouble; I will deliver him, and honor him. With long life will I satisfy him, and show him My salvation" (Psalms *91:14-16)*

Contents

		page
Chapter 1	*Live for the supernatural*	1
Chapter 2	*You must persist*	5
Chapter 3	*Move forward without fear*	10
Chapter 4	*Miracles of every kind*	13
Chapter 5	*No person is put in your path by accident*	17
Chapter 6	*Everything in life counts*	23
Chapter 7	*Against all odds*	26
Chapter 8	*Attach yourself to God*	30
Chapter 9	*Wait for the sense of peace*	33
Chapter 10	*Don't force things*	35
Chapter 11	*Rise out of self*	39
Chapter 12	*'Live in the Voice of God'*	41
Chapter 13	*Don't limit yourself*	46
Chapter 14	*Place on your lips the words, 'thank you, Jesus'*	50
Chapter 15	*The prophecy of intuition*	53
Chapter 16	*The Lord's inklings prepare us*	56
Chapter 17	*God hears every thought and sees every tear*	60
Chapter 18	*Signs and confirmations*	62
Chapter 19	*In His Name you can heal*	68
Chapter 20	*Often, it is evil that causes illness*	72
Chapter 21	*Step back from your 'test'*	75
Chapter 22	*'Unlove' is the road to darkness*	77
Chapter 23	*God knows everything that could happen*	81
Chapter 24	*'How could it be raining everywhere but here?'*	84
Chapter 25	*The light through the window*	90

page

Chapter 26 *Magnify and multiply*   95

Chapter 27 *There is no situation from which God is absent*   98

Chapter 28 *Remember that God often waits until the last moment*   101

Chapter 29 *'Illuminated by shafts of light'*   108

Chapter 30 *God wants you to enhance the dignity of others*   113

Chapter 31 *Let your abilities blossom*   115

Chapter 32 *Don't drink of the poison*   121

Chapter 33 *The real root of all evil*   127

Chapter 34 *Don't give the devil a foothold*   133

Chapter 35 *God changes our plans because He has a better one*   136

Chapter 36 *The prayer of 'desperation'*   138

Chapter 37 *Faith without love is vain*   142

Chapter 38 *Only in His Name do we pray*   145

Chapter 39 *Thankfulness works the miracle*   150

Chapter 40 *Turn fear into the energy of action*   152

Chapter 41 *We overcome when we persevere*   154

Chapter 42 *Let go and let God*   160

Chapter 43 *Don't limit the blessings God has in store for you*   166

Chapter 44 *The secret formula is a race to His embrace*   170

           Notes   185

Chapter 1

Live for the supernatural

You are a supernatural being. You are not physical. You live forever. Once you realize this – truly accept it into your heart – you will transcend all sorrow.

Not that there won't be moments of sadness, trials, and even trauma. No. But as you will see, there is tremendous evidence for the existence of the soul and the miracles that attend it. This is because there is the existence of God.

In fact, *you* are a miracle. In our current society we are so oriented toward the physical that we have lost sight of who, what, and where we really are. Because what we normally see are just the bolts and nuts, we have decided that these nuts and bolts – the wood we touch, the metal we drive, the flesh we feel, our *bodies* — are the very definition of life.

Yet the truth is that physical existence is but one dimension in God's design. In fact, your body is just a vehicle that your soul is using on earth. Beyond and above is a spiritual existence that opens up to us upon death. That existence, the spiritual side, is the realm in which there is more direct contact with God. It is what we should always keep in mind, and must always keep in touch with. It is good to put matters into perspective, and the perspective is that the average person in the West lives to be nearly eighty. The most recent statistics put life expectancy in the U.S. at 77.4 years (and rising).

That means the average person lives more than 4,000 weeks, or 28,251 days. Each of those days, and each of those seconds, has been ordained by God. We can even watch it tick on our clocks. If you are in the average range, you'll spend nearly 41 million minutes on this place called earth. It is a place that God seeks to transform into goodness.

Touch your head, hands, or arms. Move your foot. Feel the beat of your heart. This is your vehicle, how you navigate the physical dimension for those forty million minutes. Above it and organizing it is the spiritual force that links us to God. This book is about that connection; nothing is more important.

For reasons that will not be available to us *until* death, we are blinded to many aspects of that spiritual connection. There are forces that obscure it. During much of life, we're asked to operate in faith, and to be fearless. Once faith is put into action, an entirely new existence opens before us.

Such is the topic of this book: what life is about and where it leads – which, as we will see, is the miraculous, or what some call eternity.

We live forever. It's a simple truth that is demonstrated through God's abundant miracles. Did you know that? Did you know that God always wants to let you touch Him? Did you know that He always wants a miracle for you, and works them constantly? Although we rarely see it, there is a constant interplay between the "natural" and the "supernatural." Odds are you're affected every day in some way by a circumstance or event that has no earthly origin. Odds are *also* that for the most part you don't realize it. Our bodies are controlled by the soul and the soul is controlled by the spirit, which comes from the higher force of God. Your spirit is the real *you* and it knows no time, at least not time as we on earth measure it.

Getting in touch with that spirit and living for God (instead of for the natural) is the key to happiness. As we will see, there are many spiritual laws, and this is one of them: the touch of God, the miraculous, leads to happiness. A major, life-affecting rule it is. How many of you find yourselves depressed on occasion? How many fear death? How many have encountered situations that caused a loss of hope?

God never wants you to fear or despair. There is no reason for it.

Granted, all of us must endure trials from time to time. But we *never* have to endure them in desperation. A desperate or fearful response is a response that is not in tune with the miraculous, and I hope this book changes that.

In our time, most are not in touch with the God of Miracles. A large majority of people believes in Him and a majority even attends church on a regular basis (nearly half go every Sunday), but when it comes to daily life, that aspect is shoved aside. We live in a world that is devoid of the miraculous.

This is a term Jesus used — the *world* — and it means those who consider everything in terms only of what they can see, hear, taste, touch, or smell. Such people also tend to consider the brain to be the highest cognitive force. As a result, they gear everything to the systems that man has created, considering science a sort of religion instead of what it really is: just one tool of observation, and a very limited one, while we are on earth.

We have distanced ourselves from the miraculous because we are overly "scientized," if that can be a verb, and in some way I hope this book changes that for you. These days, we consider nothing true unless it is documented in a laboratory. We want to see something – including God — before believing it, while what He asks is the opposite: that we believe before seeing the results.

It gets back to the spiritual law of faith, which is a key to a supernatural life, along with love.

Meanwhile, we live with a remarkably narrow view of life. To us, existence is our homes, our families, the bedrooms in which we awaken, the bathrooms we use, the stairs. It's the trees in our yards, our cars, the buildings that blur by (on the way to work). We hardly think of the supernatural, and as a result, we feel helpless — at the mercy of those physical surroundings. The car can careen off the road. It can hit a building. It can hit one of those trees. It's as if each day is a toss of the dice. This causes fear. There is a huge, capricious element to life. We go through it hoping the dice don't turn up against us.

As I will show, such is a life of defeat because it is a life lived for the world instead of for God. When we live for Him, on the other hand, we are not at the mercy of the world, and are privy to a constant stream of wonders. While we are constantly affected by the natural, it should never be the controlling force, and we must realize that. When we live for the God of Miracles, we learn that in the scheme of eternity, the world is less real than what comes after it. Though most treat earth as if it is the whole of existence, in actuality it is but a momentary, passing phase that God puts us through in order to effect development. He explained this through the life of His Son Jesus.

The world is placed before us as a lesson and a place where we are tested and where we must be like Christ: fearless. Life is a test. Once we acknowledge this, we transcend it. Financial disorder? Emotional hurts? Sickness? What you encounter in life is often put there for your benefit – to strengthen you, to open your eternal eyes — and if you treat it that way (instead of sinking into despair), you not only shake off the gloom but resolve the problem. Put another way, a miracle occurs.

Through the years, in speaking with hundreds of scientists, I have witnessed the way a strictly scientific approach can quash the spirit. Most scientists are good men who diligently practice a certain intellectual discipline. In doing so, however, they have become so wrapped up in the details, many of them, that they have developed spiritual blindness. They even tend toward atheism — they see a physical cause for everything — and the same can happen to us: when we are obsessed with details, we wander into a forest and see only the twigs and branches and not the entire landscape.

Objects, possessions, even relationships? When we become too wrapped up in those, we lose sight of the big picture, which is that life on earth is but a prelude to life eternal and that God is right there all of the way.

It is living for eternity that is addressed by this book, a modest work, yes, but hopefully one in which you will find some personal benefit. I suggest that the examples be read in small pieces that can be meditated upon, perhaps a chapter or two at a time, or at least reviewed after a first sitting. Take your time with this book. If it takes you a couple of weeks to finish, that's fine. I believe that by meditating on the meaning behind each miracle, we are brought to see more than we normally would, and to draw closer to God. As the preacher for the Pontifical Household in Rome himself noted recently, a third of the Gospels are focused on Christ's miracles, and there was a reason for that. The reason is that each miracle carried a lesson.

Why should we live for the eternal? Is there really any proof of an afterlife? And miracles. Where? When? Who? How?

Can I really find happiness? How do I prepare for Heaven now? And in the meantime, can I be healed? Can I find peace of mind?

The answer is yes to all of the above and is what this book seeks to address. Your life can become a life of miracles. When we live for God, Who *is* the supernatural, life becomes better. There is joy even in trials. It is no longer so physical. We are no longer limited by worldliness.

It is when we live for the other world – when we become *otherworldly* – that a new dimension opens, and as you will see, it is then that the miraculous materializes.

Chapter 2

You must persist

Take the case of George Bamba, a former senator in Guam who contracted AIDS from a blood transfusion. In 1996, Bamba was in the middle of a campaign for re-election when he was diagnosed after severe "flu" and asthma symptoms. Unconscious when he arrived at the hospital, Bamba woke up days later to the death sentence.

The doctor came in, paced around nervously, and then returned when Bamba's wife and daughter had left, explaining that he had a type pneumonia contracted because of HIV. There was no T-cell count, which gauges the body's ability to destroy infected cells, and because of that, he was given just thirty days to live.

But Bamba refused to accept the "evil report," and at each step, he fought against the judgment of this world. It was a war that went on not for days but for eight *years*. The Filipino was to beat back a constant onslaught. Against the odds he defeated that bout of pneumonia and began an incredible fight based on faith. Prayers and anointing with blessed oil from Carmelites helped him to overcome any number of side effects – even causing an intestinal blockage to disappear, astonishingly enough, before major surgery. But that was hardly the end of his struggles. He was on morphine. He was taking 36 pills a day. There were countless times that Bamba was so sick they could not even register a pulse.

In 2003, after seven years of suffering, he appeared to be at the end of his rope. The battle now was with hepatitis C, which was deemed "incurable." Bamba's liver was in failure. Each day he counted his quality time in *minutes*. With doctors unable to do anything, Bamba turned to something called the "precious Bible promises"and with it he overcame the hepatitis. But *still*, the war had not yet been won. He needed an operation to bolster his weakened heart and had to contend with a cyst on his kidney!

It didn't look good. Once more, the end seemed in sight. Doctors didn't expect much. But there was a "voice" that kept saying, "Wait!" And there were the continued prayers. At one point Bamba was in such pain (the disease was attacking his nerve endings) that he begged his doctor to amputate his left leg! His wife brought him a Bible and Bamba read it from cover to cover. Little by little, Scripture began to work its power. "The more I read," recalled the politician, "the stronger I became physically." This tenacity caused the miracle. In June, two months after failing a treadmill test, he now passed a second exam and felt no more pains in his chest. The heart problem had faded and his other organs had strengthened. He started to feel *well*. By 2004, at age 52, he was free of HIV — "feeling better than even before he was diagnosed with AIDS," noted a newspaper — and astonishingly, no longer taking medication!

A "miracle" (actually a series of miracles) had occurred. His life became wondrous due to the attributes we will discuss: faith, persistence, patience, prayer, and closeness to God. Let's also toss in fearlessness.

I have seen dozens of other healings, some even more dramatic. In Boston an executive named Art Boyle had cancer of the kidney which had spread to his lungs, normally a death sentence. Yet Boyle too refused to accept the evil report, shook off the fear, put stock in prayer, and had a woman known for her closeness to God lay hands on him.

The next time there was a CAT scan, the lung nodule was gone.

On Long Island was a woman named Sandy who had such extensive cancer that doctors sent her home to die with a prescription for morphine.

Although not very religious, Sandy asked a priest for help and he suggested that she pray for the intercession of a certain saint that she couldn't remember after the priest left.

But she prayed, calling out for the help of *any* saint, and that night, September 4, 2001, she claims that Therese the Little Flower, the Catholic saint connected to so many miracles, appeared in front of her.

"I was just sitting on the couch and all of a sudden I smelled this pretty, rose-like smell, and then I looked up a little bit and I could see St. Therese, and she was kind of glimmering, but the more I looked at her, the more solid she became," says Sandy – who didn't know it was Therese until later, when she saw a holy card. "At the beginning I was actually a bit frightened and amazed at the same time. I didn't ask her anything. She said she was here and she came to heal me. She told me that Jesus had a special purpose for me and that was the reason she was healing me, that I had special work. I had these lumps on my arms and everything, and this tumor on my hip, and they went away. I was on all these medicines, including morphine, *but I'm not taking anything now.*"

On one occasion, she said, hundreds of rose petals materialized, as if from thin air.

These are not "nut cases." They are people who exercised a number of principles and saw God respond lavishly.

As we will see time and again, the key to living miraculously is to love in all circumstances; to believe with an ever-living faith; to surrender beyond trust; to hope beyond hope; to release all pride; to persevere beyond endurance; and to keep our eyes on the God of miracles.

I spoke to another man who had incurable brain tumors. Two were above his eyes and tests showed that the tissue between his brain and skull was suffused with a web-like growth – a cancer — that covered the top of his brain.

Not a promising diagnosis. The pain was such that Jeff Thummel of Midland, Texas, was up all but an hour or two a night. To get rest, he would get out of bed and try soaking in a hot bath, to little avail. No medication would touch it. "It was like a coal burning in my head," he told me. "About a hundred times a day I'd get like a shock going from my ear and out the right eye or right temple."

But there were people praying for him, a lot of people, prayer lines, and one night Jeff settled down to watch the first game of the basketball playoffs, lying on his couch. Usually he could do that for only thirty seconds and then the pounding would start. He figured he'd have to watch most of the game sitting up or even standing. But for some reason he lay down on the couch, fell asleep, and when he awoke much later, at 4:30 a.m., *he didn't have a headache.* Nor was there a headache the next day. Here he was ready for surgery and the symptoms no longer existed! "So I called the doctor and left a message on his nurse's machine saying that during my pre-work for brain surgery I wanted another MRI done, because something had physically changed and I wanted to confirm that," says Jeff.

All but ignoring his request, the medical professionals argued that they were "110 percent sure" tumors were there and had to come out. "She called back on Monday morning and somewhat sarcastically said, 'What do you think happened, a *miracle*?'" he recounts.

Prayers were stepped up. Jeff persisted. He carried a picture of St. John Neumann (a former bishop whose tomb is visited by many who claim miracles) and asked for the intercession of St. Padre Pio. He also went to a prayer group, where he was anointed with holy oil.

And then the day of surgery came. This was at the Southwest Medical Center in Dallas – a no-nonsense, "prestigious" place.

Thummel says he took the oil with him and placed two images of St.

Neumman under the heels of his feet — in case the nurses took away the image he was carrying with him.

The surgery was expected to take 12 to 14 hours but only part of the way through Jeff found himself awake and in intensive care instead of the operating room.

"I thought something had gone very wrong. The doctor was standing beside me.

"But he said they were through and that things had gone 'very well.'"

Well, indeed!

When they had opened Jeff up, nothing was there.

No tumors.

So astonished were the doctors that they sent samples to a national center for disease – which confirmed that the disease was gone.

There is also the recent case of Colleen Willard from the Chicago suburbs. Colleen's case is so noteworthy that her doctors have prepared testimonies for the Vatican.

Like Bamba, she had a laundry list of serious ailments. There was what's called Hashimoto's thyroiditis. There was myofascial fibromyalgia. There was severe osteomalacia. There was a critical adrenal insufficiency. Most significant was a hypothalamic growth.

Again, a brain tumor.

"It was inoperable tumor and sat right in front of the hypothalamus gland next to the major blood vessel in the brain," says Colleen, who was treated by specialists at the famed Mayo Clinic. "We asked them how much time I had and they told me the tumor was in my 'soul' — that the hypothalamus is the major gland that regulates the heart, the lungs, everything in your body, and that they could not even do a biopsy — it would have been life-threatening. They said that what they would find is that cancer would show up as a secondary tumor somewhere.

"We talked about the growth and how they could not actually operate because I might turn out to be a vegetable."

In desperate need, but unwilling to give up, Colleen decided to take a religious pilgrimage and did so despite the opposition of all those doctors, who didn't think she could survive the trip. She was on oxygen. She could hardly speak for more than several minutes at a stretch. Her suffering became so extreme that she was no longer able to climb the stairs to her bedroom without assistance. Anything that touched her skin caused pain. But all of this was the prelude to a wonder.

Venturing to a place called Medjugorje (in former Yugoslavia), Colleen went to Mass and felt something leaving her body. "When the Eucharist was placed on my tongue, immediately I was aware of heat leaving, and when the heat was leaving, the pain that I had 24 hours a day started to go," recounts the woman, who was in a wheelchair. "It was at that point, after Holy Communion, that my husband looked at me and *saw* on my face what was happening. Without saying a word he got down on his knees next to the wheelchair. I said, 'John, please get me out of this wheelchair. It feels cumbersome. I can move my hands. I can move my arms! Look: there's no pain!'"

To the shock of observers, Colleen Willard was able to get out of the chair.

When she returned to Illinois, Colleen looked so good that she was hardly recognizable to her caretakers. "All my Mayo doctors declared this a miracle," says this woman, whose grave disease was gone, along with the darkness that came with it.

Chapter 3

Move forward without fear

Why persist when we are so ill? Colleen felt that the answer came from the Blessed Mother, who she said spoke to her, saying, *"God does not give you a disease and then abandon you."*

Persistence is a deeper walk of faith. When we maintain faith, persist beyond persistence (as did Christ), and hope beyond hope (as did His mother), the God of miracles is near. The smaller we are, the larger He is. Heaven hears our pleas and is with us every inch of the way.

It doesn't seem like it at times. In fact it can feel downright lonely. On occasion there is what theologians call the "dark night of the soul."

But the graces are there when we look for them.

Nothing in life – no matter how "bad" – *is* actually bad if we take from it what God intended.

While on earth we pass through a constant series of tests, whether they are in our emotional lives, our finances, our work, our spiritual walk, or our health. God always places lessons before us, and we repeat such tests until we get them right. Then there are new tests! They mold us and cause us to evolve. We must accept this.

But such is not to say that all illness is sent because we're in need of correction. There is redemptive suffering; we follow in the path of Jesus. But many trials are related to deficiencies. Are you impatient? God may send events to make you wait. Are you unfriendly? He may plant you among people who need friends. Do you have a temper? Situations will arrive allowing you to respond gently instead of with anger.

Trials come in various ways but usually with the same theme: the development of love, caring, faith, fearlessness, and persistence.

Think of the trials in your own life and know that God does not expect us to transform over night; to get to where we need to be takes a lifetime; for the most part, Our God is a gradual One.

But at times the tests are the type that pound us into shape, more than refine us.

When, suddenly, a serious illness strikes (as in the cases I just cited), it puts other problems that we thought were so "important" into an entirely different perspective. The Lord stretches us and forges us and folds us. He holds us like metal over a flame. He presses us, heats us, puts us into water. Then he sets us in fire once more, buffs us, and applies a polish that we might be a reflection of Him.

You've heard the analogy of how gold is purified by fire. So it is with us. He molds us through trials, and once we accept that we transcend it.

With each little test, we gain grace, and grace works the wonders. Little miracles build into great ones.

They are not predictable. There are no set patterns. Some are instant. Some are very gradual. It's a matter of letting go and letting the God of miracles flow through. "Openness" is very important, and that means the persistent belief that something can happen.

When we do that, when we persist in faith, when we actually expect something to occur, we see first small miracles (answers to initial prayers) and then increasingly larger ones.

It requires a connection with God and such is accomplished by seeking repentance, forgiving others, and praying without ceasing, as Scripture advises us. The more tenacious we are, the more prone we are to grace. The more we contribute to His household, the more He opens what in *Malachi* (3:10) He calls "the windows of Heaven." (Another translation says "floodgates.")

But don't think you can pin it down to an earthly timetable. Miracles arrive in God's good time, in the way that He deems best, and most are not as dramatic as what was witnessed by Colleen Willard.

But they do come, and often we don't recognize them.

We think of our good "luck." We peg it as having a good day. Things are "going well" for us. We're on a "roll." We figure it as just part of a cycle and don't recognize the little wonders as supernatural. They seem too small to be anything but happenstance — but miracles they are. Remember this: all good fortune (truly good fortune) is Heaven-sent.

The fact that you have gotten to the point you are without succumbing to the almost infinite ways that you can be hurt in life is a testimony to protective grace. Think of all the bad things that can happen. You can drop eggs. You can scald yourself on the coffee pot. You can fall down the stairs. You can run a stop sign. You can back into someone at the deli. You can contract the flu, or something as bad as hepatitis. You can be exposed to carcinogens. You can ingest *salmonella*. You can suffer an innumerable array of internal disorders, any of which can have serious effects.

Yet every step of the way, the Lord of miracles is watching over you.

Knowing that, we then see that life is a stream of miracles and that additional ones come over time. When God approves of the way we have passed a lesson, He demonstrates His love. It is His love that spawns miracles. Often good fortune comes in a run that continues until there is an interruption or "dry" period when He doesn't seem to be listening and again is testing us.

Such can be very wrenching. It can also be frustrating. How many figures in the Bible cried out to God because He didn't seem to be listening? Even Jesus on the Cross [*Matthew* 27:46]! Yet if we fully maintain our confidence in Him – and in Christ — our progress becomes still greater.

God never fails to do what is in our best personal interest and never fails to answer a prayer in the way He deems correct. He seeks only the opening. We have to let Him in by casting out fear and replacing it with faith. "By truly understanding this and letting Light work through us, we gain sensitivity, peace, and power that we have never experienced before," notes one healer. "We become greater than we are. We understand that which is beyond the realm of reality. And then we see miracles unfold before our very eyes. *All kinds of them!*"

Chapter 4

Miracles of every kind

There are all types of miracles. They come in the way of signs, inspiration, protection, and the reversal of fortune. There are conversions. There is sudden success. A miracle is when we experience good fortune despite the odds; it always gets back to God; He can regulate life in any way He chooses, whenever He chooses; He is all and encompasses all and can do anything at a moment's notice. He may also take centuries or even millennia. That doesn't make it any less miraculous. A miracle is a precipitation of His goodness.

When we make a mistake, however small, and God rights it, that too is a miracle.

It all gets back to God, Who keeps track of every particle.

The miracles that most catch our notice are healings, and I have seen all kinds. There have been sudden cures from multiple sclerosis, heart problems, blood disease, cirrhosis, paralysis, broken bones, stomach disorders, every form of cancer, and epilepsy, as in Jesus' time. We don't understand how such healings occur. What we can say is that in our highest form, we are composed of a force called the "spirit." The spirit, which can not normally be seen, oversees the body like an organizing field. It controls everything in you. It affects every cell, and forms new ones. We are "spirit" more than we are a physical process, and our spirits originate in the Spirit of God and return like a brook to a river.

Scientists have even detected the energy around us. We see it portrayed as a halo in pictures of saints. It makes sense even if all we can see (until we die) is the physical. Did you ever wonder how the body can reconfigure itself so perfectly after an injury, or how at times we can go on with virtually no food? There have been saints who've subsisted for years on nothing but the Eucharist.

Such is the work of an unknown nonphysical power in cooperation with the physical. Although it must be approached with the greatest of caution (for it can tend toward the occult), scientists have taken photos of a mysterious surrounding force. We live in a soup of energy. According to Einstein, matter itself is energy vibrating at a lower level. In spirit, we would see objects not as solid but as a collection of widely-spaced particles. Above, between, and around those particles is the Power of God, which permeates everything and concentrates around those who pray and for whom others pray, regulating the body. It is not an impersonal force. It is an extension of the Ultimate Intelligence, one that simply wants us to love Him and be good. When we transgress His Will, we inhibit His flow by placing a block in our spirits.

Such negativity may then cause discomfort and can graduate to illness. A spiritual rule is that *negativities increase the likelihood of illness.* They attract "anti-miracles." Look at a person who is negative and you'll almost see a darkness around him. With every negativity, we bring a wisp of darkness.

Little such wisps can form into a cloud and that darkness can then transmit to the physical. It isn't just illness. When there's a "dark cloud" around a person, the negative is drawn like a magnet. Evil enters the picture. There can be accidents, problems in relationships, stubborn financial distress, and psychological unbalance, as well as sickness. It is like a self-induced curse: the physical is a reflection of the spiritual.

Thoughts are powerful. They bring the spiritual world alive around us.

Scripture informs us that "a wholesome tongue is a tree of life" (*Psalms* 52:2), while a negative one can "set the course of nature on fire" (and "defileth the whole body," says *James* 3:6).

With our tongues we can "prevail" or we can devise destruction (*Psalms* 12:4 and 52:2).

The tongue is among our strongest members. When we say things like, "It makes me sick," or "This is killing me," there can be physical repercussions.

Sin and negativity put a blot on our souls and such blots project their darkness.

Once more, such is not to say that everyone who is sick is negative! Illness is also a test of life. Often, the innocent suffer greatly. We'll understand why when we die.

But when we're negative we're placing blocks in our spirits, and our spirits – those forces around us, the forces that transcend the dimensions of the visible world, higher even than the soul – are our connection to God.

On the other hand, exercising goodness, doing God's Will, and especially having faith ("trust beyond trust"), removes the "blots" and opens channels.

It is when such channels are open that healing occurs.

Look at the example of Jesus. In most cases, before He cured someone, first He had to cast out demons!

Thus: we can say that before there are miracles (whether healing or something else we need) we have to reduce the darkness. Often this occurs through simple repentance. When we seek forgiveness, our humility touches God and moves Him to action. Repentance acknowledges the God of all creation and is an active statement that we want to change our ways to conform with His intent for the cosmos. Whether or not it happens right away, repentance shows an intent that gets the process of miracles, the flow of grace, in motion. When we are operating in the miraculous, we seek forgiveness at the same time that we forgive others.

Note that one definition of forgiveness is a renouncement of anger.

Through repentance, we are cutting the connection to hatefulness.

When we seek forgiveness, we are also acknowledging our subservience to One True God.

God and only God can effect true miracles.

Confession is the brilliant sacrament for this, and grants us a fresh chance to reorient, although at times it takes trials and sufferings, which have a cleansing effect. To get our attention, God sometimes allows drastic events. Paul had to be blinded before he could see. We need a "jolt." There is a man named Robert Morales in Austin, Texas, who was working as a lineman's assistant when he touched a live, 7,200-volt cable. He seemed like a goner – electrocuted, hanging on that tower — but he called out to God, repented profoundly (if hastily), and suddenly found himself flung back in such a way that the flow of current halted. He went on to convert and become a lay evangelist (who reports miracles of healing).

I also spoke to a man named David Gant, who got trapped in an underwater cave in Tennessee while scuba diving (or "spelunking") and was saved only after he was spiritually cleansed and only after his own exercise in persistence.

Imagine his quandary: there he was in a dark cave, trying to breathe in an air bubble that was rapidly being depleted of its oxygen.

It was August 15, 1992. Dave and friends had been spearing catfish. Now he was all alone in a water-filled cavern known as Nickajack. He was lost in the cave, trapped for more than 14 hours, before he said his first prayers. He too was sure he was a goner. All he had to hold onto was a piece of stalactite in the exhausting effort to keep his head above water.

Finally, Gant went to God, repented, and that's all it took.

He encountered an incredible sensation.

"I asked the Lord to come into my life to save my soul, and He did it, just like *that*," he said. "It felt like a big invisible hand went straight in my chest all the way to my toes and pulled out evil – pure evil. Three different times, one after the other. Three times. After the first time I didn't think I could feel any better — I felt so *clean*. After the second time I felt just that much cleaner — and after the third time it's a wonder that cave didn't cave in, I was shouting so loud, echoing in that cavern, just praising the Lord for what He just did for me! I felt so clean. I have never felt so clean and so *alive,* so happy, in my life!"

Here he was dying – ready to suffocate in the cold dark, to descend into a watery grave – and David felt better than he ever had.

Cleansed, and praising God, he was now ready for a miracle. It was at this point that he *suddenly saw a strange fog directly in front of him.* It was slightly luminous, just light enough to see, and inside, he said, were what looked like four oblong objects. They and the fog were slowly moving away. It's not clear what they were, but now, more than twenty hours after he got lost, there was a sudden roaring sound that sent bubbles up to replenish the air pocket. There was more oxygen! And soon a pair of rescue divers appeared to escort him to safety.

Evil had been removed and was followed by a miracle.

The way out of the cave turned out to be the same route, by the way, that the "fog" had taken.

Chapter 5

No person is put in your path by accident

God is watching you, no matter how deep down (or up to your neck) you are. In fact, He is closer than your shadow.

"When I was about thirteen years old, I had gone swimming with my Girl Scout troop," noted Martha Anne Drolet of Rhode Island. "Although I didn't know how to swim, my friends teased me into jumping off the deep end of the pool. Don't ask me why I did it, but foolishly I jumped in and found myself sinking and struggling to rise to the top for air. I kept going under and finally couldn't surface any longer! I remember sinking and fighting to stay alive. Suddenly, I felt an indescribable peace come over me, and I just gave up struggling. I found myself in what seemed to be an incredibly bright whirlpool or tunnel. I was at total peace. The light was blindingly bright, and I saw my entire life go before my eyes."

The next thing Martha knew, she was at the topside of the pool, not knowing how she got there. Someone had saved her, but no one saw anything.

She had been saved by God, Who watches every speck of His creation. He is aware of every subatomic particle in every component of every atom and watches each spin of an electron in the same way that He knows each motion of every planet. Does He really watch over every person? There is nothing that can occur in your body, down to the tiniest biochemical reaction, in the smallest cell, of which He is not cognizant.

This is truly miraculous. He is aware of every grain of sand. He can watch a cell like He can watch a galaxy. All the forces of the world, whether magnetism, gravity, nuclear forces, or electricity, are but branches of a vastly larger power that springs from a small part of Him. At will, God can control or suspend any one of them. This He may do so slowly, over the course of centuries (escaping our notice), or faster than a second. His miracles are a manipulation of "normal" forces and this He effects directly or through the use of agents.

The Lord of miracles is with everyone and everything, everywhere, at all times, and every creature – every single one – is a miracle.

Once I was driving in St. Augustine, Florida, and I passed a construction site where there was this big mound of sand. I thought of how many grains there were in that one pile. It would take a monumental effort for a scientist to get a real count (if such is even practical). Then I thought of how many grains there were in the neighborhood. The pile was set on just one lot; there were probably a dozen or more lots on just that side of the street. A few blocks away is the beach. Can you imagine how many grains are there? The beach is more than a hundred yards wide and many feet deep.

Now imagine how many grains there are in that whole city, county, and state. Then think a moment about how many grains there would be on every beach in the whole world, on every desert, and anywhere else that has sand.

I saw one estimate of four billion *billion*.

Another put it at a million times that.

In the human body, there are between ten and 100 trillion cells.

To God, these are trivial numbers.

It's beyond our ability to count, and yet *God is aware of every single one of those cells.*

There is no hiding: He is aware not only of who you are and every thing you have done and of every thought you have had. He is waiting for you to go to Him but no one is beyond His help. I hear from folks whose darkest depressions have disappeared overnight, or who have actually felt a hand save them (who claimed that someone grabbed them as they tumbled off a ledge, or whose steering wheel felt like it was turned by an unseen hand, preventing an accident; this happened to me).

A miracle is a manifestation of His love.

He withdraws from us to test us and shows Himself through miracles when He wants to remind us of Who He is.

Why must we have faith? He tests us for those things the fallen angels lacked. They lacked trust. They did not persist. They refused to serve. They would not love. God seeks to know what is in our own hearts, and wants us to follow the way of His Son. In Jesus were the attributes that led to miracles. Mercy. Purity. Love. Trust beyond trust – and beyond the grave. When we are like Jesus, we are like the Father, and He opens to us. Jesus was the personification of God's miraculous side. When He is quiet, He is either testing us or waiting for us to invite Him.

Most often, He is subtle. When His grace flows, we have a good day. Things go our way. If we are heading to shop in another city, the sky is clear, the air is fresh, it's busy downtown, but we spot a parking space on the street right near the store so we don't have to pay at a garage and don't have far to walk. We get what we need; the price is reasonable; they can ship it for us; the sales clerk is friendly; the drive home is a breeze. Don't slough that off. It's a miracle. It is the touch of "grace." Our mistake? We think of it as "luck." The world is so big, many figure, that certain events are bound to occur in a remarkable pattern. They are simply a matter time. They call it the "law of truly large numbers," which states that with a large enough sample, with a big enough array of people, coincidences are bound to happen.

In our hyper-scientific world, just about everything remarkable is now chalked up to the "luck" of the draw. I have seen scientists explain away some truly astonishing phenomena by resorting to that common rationale. In the news of the moment is a man named Stewart Petrie who lost his wedding ring while clamming in Long Island Sound. A former doctor, Petrie described the area as half the size of a football field, with four feet of water and muck and sand at the bottom. He lost the ring – an emblem of his forty years of marriage – in 2003, and he was devastated. Two years later, Petrie returned to the same area for some clamming, something he only does a couple of times a year — and along with some clams, he brought home an encrusted, almost copper-looking ring that got caught in his rake. "Wouldn't it be funny if it was your ring?" his wife said, as she went into the bathroom to wash it off.

With a little bit of scrubbing and jewelry cleaner, she could see her inscription: "MPS to SJP 9-10-67."

This was not a coincidence. It was orchestrated by the Lord, as are all good things in our lives. When we die, when we see with spiritual eyes, we'll be amazed at God's tapestry. Perhaps I should say "needlepoint." With needlepoint one side looks like just a bunch of ugly knotted threads, which don't make sense, while the reverse side is a piece of art.

That's how our lives are. The physical is a shadow of the spiritual. On earth, we see the knotted threads. In Heaven, we'll see with new eyes (at death our perception will become far clearer) and we'll find that every minute of our lives, every event, and every person we encountered was there for a purpose. We all have a unique purpose, and we weave in and out of each other's lives in a large miraculous plan.

Before we were knitted in the womb, God knew us, says *Psalms* 139:13, and our interactions are extremely important. Only when we die will we understand why everything and everyone have happened onto our paths.

No person is put in our way by accident. In every case, those we meet, even for the briefest time, have crossed our paths for a reason. Think of the people in your life, those who are relatives, who tended to you as a baby in the hospital, who taught you, who were friends or schoolmates or acquaintances (don't neglect to recall strangers). Think of everyone with whom you have worked or worshipped or passed at the checkout – every person you have encountered. In a way that's mysterious, all were put there for a reason.

We meet people to help each other develop, and when we react positively, it builds toward the miraculous. Just about every challenge in life, every problem, every hurdle, is a test of love, and God keeps sending us opportunities as He sharpens us against hard surfaces. When we respond to difficulty with love, all of Heaven cheers. Every person has an equal role in God's plan of love and endless opportunities to express that love. *If we want miracles, we have to be a miracle to others.*

I once interviewed a woman from Long Island named Barbara who had a near-death experience during exploratory surgery for endometriosis, a female reproductive disorder. She is another of those who had technically "died." "They told my husband they had lost me and didn't know if they could get me back," recounted Barbara, who found herself out of her body, beyond the operating room, and in the presence of an extraordinary light. "The first thing that happened was that I realized I was in a void. It was a total black place in space, and for a fraction of a second, I was very scared.

"But as quickly as that came, I was directed to the left side of me, and as soon as I turned, there appeared a Light in the distance to the left side which immediately comforted me.

"At that point I just started heading toward that Light with my being (I don't know how) and I was surrounded by what I would describe as a tunnel," continued Barbara. "There were like rings of wind, like the funnel of a tornado, and it was moving forward. Besides the Light, which was very bright, there was a prism and music unlike any that there is on earth. I don't know how to explain it. The music was so welcoming, so comforting, and so angelic that it became a part of you. I was moving up this tunnel and getting closer to the Light and I know there was some kind of companion with me, because every time that I thought to ask a question, everything was immediately answered. I remember briefly stopping because within the walls of this tunnel were *beings*. I didn't have a great religious upbringing and never thought of purgatory, but when I came back it seemed like part of that, probably the last level of purgatory. The souls existed on the outside of the tunnel and were resting, as if they were sitting or standing or lying down.

"The light was brilliant. You can't describe its brilliance. It was just filled with love, peace, and the knowledge of God. As you move through that tunnel, you're more and more consumed by it. And then I was in the Presence of the Lord. I was prostrate. I was not able to withstand the majesty and the awesomeness of what was before me! I was nothingness compared to that. And then there was a period of being embraced by this love and peace and serenity and knowing I had reached my final destination, that this was truly a home."

There was also a review of her life. Call it Barbara's judgment. *And she found it astonishing to see the needlepoint.*

Especially wondrous was how her life had interwoven with others.

What Barbara thought as small achievements in her life – barely remembered – were magnificent to God. She was shown the day she had spent time listening to an acquaintance who had lost her fiancé in a car accident. This was crucial to Christ; it was one of the highlights of Barbara's life, and she didn't even know it. She was also shown the time she had placed her hand on the shoulder of a woman grieving at church.

Christ considered this one of her great achievements in life — just that little gesture, just that *moment,* and when we see life from that perspective, we realize that every person we encounter is meant to be encountered and is often set there as an opportunity for us to become a little miracle. It is not great feats the Lord is looking for — not feats as men describe great feats; it is how much we help others. It is how we make each other feel. It is kindness. It is the personal touch.

"When you see it through the eyes of the Lord, you see your life as a *whole,"* emphasized the Long Island woman. "You see how in the course of all creation your life makes a difference and you see how it affected the Creator — how it stops at the Creator when you offend one of His own.

"We don't see things the way the Lord does, and for me it was a tremendous eye-opener. At this point the way I was offending the Lord the most in my life was my attitude and the way I spoke to my husband and children — my nearly verbal abuse. It was the tone and the things that I said that were very offending to another's soul and heart. You can be firm with your kids, but the Lord doesn't want you to use an insulting tone. I was shown my vocabulary and the tone with which I said things, because it was a condescending one."

In this trip to the other side, Barbara was shown how particular events bore tremendous repercussions. When she rose grumpily from sleep and was negative to her family, she saw how this spread to others throughout the day — at school, at the workplace, at stores — and then through the families of those who were touched by the negativity.

She was shown a drop of light that started in one spot and went around the globe in the band of light. That was the way it was supposed to be. But she was also shown that when she awoke and was negative, a circle of darkness went over the circle of light, erasing it. "When I got up in the morning, smiled, and presented breakfast, hugging the children, it went from my house everywhere," said Barbara. "I was shown a drop of light that falls into this ocean and has a rippling effect."

We have more of an effect on the world with our everyday lives than we realize, Barb's experience showed. God wants us to create goodness. In this way are we little co-miracle-workers. The goodness we present to our families will spread at work or to a guy at the deli who then conveys it to others who take it home to disseminate in a chain reaction that doesn't stop — that seems, at least in the spirit, to have miraculously global consequences.

Chapter 6

Everything in life counts

From such reports we learn that everything in life counts. There may be elements of luck, but more likely the scheme of eternity is so vast that every single thing has meaning. It only *looks* like coincidence because we can't see the big picture. God is the God of miracles and He is also the God of coincidence.

Marvel at the family in which you were born, the way your children are, the friends placed in your path, the way your career formed. When we realize all the ways we could have missed meeting our spouses, our employers, or a group of dear friends, we begin to detect something more at work than the capricious forces of nature; we begin to see the stage on which miracles occur.

Often, God's grace is most evident in coincidence. There is the hairdresser who introduces you to a customer who introduces you to a babysitter you desperately needed. There's the carpenter who turns out to be the perfect one for the project you wanted. There's the doctor who is just the right doctor, at the right time – who just happened to be on duty.

Back when I was in my first year of college another freshman stopped me as I was about to enter the campus center. He asked if I had a match. At the time, both of us were smokers. I had a match, we became friends, and he ended up marrying my twin sister.

Odds are God doesn't approve of smoking, but He designed the fact that our paths would cross.

Sometimes it's even more direct. I'll give you the example of meeting my *own* wife. For years – many frustrating ones – I'd hoped for the right woman to come along, but by the time I was forty, that still had not occurred. I began to recite daily prayers to that effect. For several years, despite discouragement, I persevered.

One evening I walked into my bedroom and heard the phone ringing. It was my business line, and I usually ignored it after dinner.

But "something" made me pick it up — it sounded insistent — and at the other end was a woman with an unusually vibrant voice. She said she had just read one of my books and was going to write me but instead found my number and called. Later she explained she'd had a "prompt" telling her to call instead of penning a letter. *"Pick up the phone."* She said she had then called my publisher, who as a matter of policy never gave out my number (which at the time was unlisted), but happened to reach an employee who gave it to her.

We talked, hung up, and afterward, she began to pray when she "heard" the prompt again. This time it was simply, *"Matthew 19:6."*

"Coincidentally," that's the passage (*"what God has put together..."*) about marriage!

We were married six months later and I never did discover who the "employee" was.

All of us have such examples.

Remember when Jesus told His followers to go to the sea, throw in a hook, and take up the first fish they caught? He told them when they opened its mouth, there would be a coin (*Matthew* 17:27), and there was. It was a sign He had orchestrated, as He also orchestrates them for us. The more we meditate on what God has done, the more He does.

The miraculous is there for the asking. There are exceptions. There are those trials of life. But God loves to operate in the realm of "luck." If you think back over your life, you'll be hit with a steady stream of luck that changed your life. That's where we see God working many of His miracles. As the saying goes, coincidence is God's way of remaining anonymous, and the dictionary tells us that coincidence is "a sequence of events that although accidental seems to have been planned or arranged" – which is correct about the events being "arranged" but wrong about them being "accidental."

There is the house that becomes available when we are looking for a house or the mailman who shows up with a letter from a friend who is on your mind or the person on the street who just happens to know the location of the out-of-the-way place you're looking for. One of the more astonishing cases was that of a man from the state of Washington who was in the music ministry – and thinking of quitting. On the road and staying overnight in Dayton, Ohio, he was walking up a strange street looking to buy a Pepsi when he passed a payphone that started ringing — at that very moment.

At first startled, then hesitant, this man decided to pick up the public phone and found that an operator was on the other end making a person-to-person call and asking for someone by his name!

So out of the blue and unlikely was this that he thought he was on

Candid Camera.

He was not. The operator was putting through a call from an emotionally distraught woman who once had seen the musician on TV and was now contemplating suicide. She had been desperately praying to find him and explained that the number she had dialed – the payphone — flashed into her mind in a vision. "Coincidentally," it was the number of the phone he was passing, and after talking to him, she changed her mind about suicide. "What are the odds of that?" he asked. "A billion to one?"

Perhaps a bit more than that.

Anyway, she lived and he stayed in ministry.

Chapter 7

Against all odds

There are times prayers aren't "answered" – at least not in the way we want. But when we're in tune with God there's often a confluence of events that works in our favor. We are not all privy to "major" miracles. We can go our entire lives without witnessing something like that pay phone. But we are all recipients of blessings, which are "minor" miracles, and they grow the more we are in tune with how God works in our daily lives. Being in touch with the God of miracles has nothing to do with extraordinary wonders but rather with the blessings that propel us through our earthly "exile."

Want to talk about odds? There was the woman from Baltimore who aspired to do a Christian musical. Three weeks after praying that God would send her the necessary resources, she won $76 million in a lottery.

Does God approve of gambling? Not really. But He can use what He wants to help us, to reward us, and most of all, to further His work. *Service is very important.* Whenever you have been blessed, ask yourself what God wants you to do with that blessing.

Blessings especially come in the way of protection. When you think of all the ways you could be harmed in the simple course of a day and how many things could go wrong with your body — how your life, one of those 100 trillion cells, could fall into chaos at a moment's notice — you begin to appreciate the blessed side of existence. The fact that we get by each day is due to grace that goes largely unrecognized.

The Lord of miracles not only permeates your body and causes all to function in proper order but also does this throughout the universe. Everything meshes in a way that is far beyond accident. In fact, accidents play no part of it. Do you realize that an extremely slight difference in the strength of nuclear reactions would prevent stars from exploding into the supernovas that spread elements like carbon and oxygen – substances essential for life – across the universe and that if what is known as the "strong" nuclear force were just half a percent stronger or weaker, stars could not make carbon – the building block of life – in the first place?

To believe that this was all generated randomly is preposterous. A living thing cannot grow from nothing. When we look at a seed that seems nothing like a plant and then see that with soil, water, and sunlight it grows into a unique life form, we put labels on it like "photosynthesis" and accept that as gospel when in fact what we have witnessed is a miracle. It came from God, Who is the force that creates, permeates, organizes, and holds everything together. That is why He can instantly change a physical situation, transforming the very character of something or precipitating something physical from "nothing." He does this at a level we won't be able to see until we are on the other side of the "needlepoint." Meanwhile, science cannot describe that and a million other processes. It can't answer many questions: What is the universe made of? What is the biological basis for consciousness? What controls organ regeneration? How can a skin cell become a nerve cell? How does a single somatic cell become a whole plant?

Think of the many minute processes in your body that can go out of whack: enzymes, white blood cells, your sugar level, the processes in the liver, your kidneys, the functioning of your entire digestive and circulatory and coronary and nervous systems, with all the attendant cells and chemicals. In God's grace, they intermesh and (when we mesh with Him) are protected.

When God wants to protect something, He doesn't care about the rules of physics. He can transcend them on any level. A former director of the National Hurricane Center (and an active Christian), Dr. Neil Frank, recalled a hurricane called Betsy that swerved away from hitting its original targets. A huge storm, more than 600 miles from edge to edge, with an "eye" estimated to be forty miles in breadth, Betsy aimed for South Carolina and Virginia but whirled to a stop about 350 miles east of Jacksonville as thousands prayed it away. The next day, when it started moving again, it had reversed direction, startling the experts.

The same thing happened in 2002 when New Orleans was threatened. Twice in one week, hurricanes veered away from that city where so many prayed and where they invoked the Blessed Mother as a miracle-worker known as Our Lady of Prompt Succor. One of them, Lili, went from a 145 to 70 miles an hour overnight, sparing New Orleans at the last moment. "SCIENTISTS DON'T YET KNOW WHY LILI SUDDENLY COLLAPSED," blared a headline.

Many were the accounts after Hurricane Katrina of statues or crucifixes that stood where nothing else did, or of Holy Water that seemed to protect homes from the destruction that was otherwise around them. "I met someone who told me his brother lives in Biloxi and evacuated their house and as they left said to a statue of Our Lady in the backyard, 'dear Blessed Mother, please protect our house,' a simple prayer, and when they flew over a few days later, all the homes were obliterated but their home was standing and missing only three shingles and Our Lady was still standing beautifully in the back," one woman informed me.

When tornadoes tore through Kissimmee, Florida, in 1998, with 220-mile-an-hour winds, a Bible was the only thing left in one devastated trailer — on top of the rubble, "looking almost new," noted a newspaper. The same occurred in LaPlata, Maryland, when a powerful F-5 leveled a Catholic school but spared the tabernacle. In Deltona, Florida, a fire devastated Faith Baptist Church and once more the only thing that wasn't melted, charred, or destroyed by water was the Bible lying on a table.

The relevant scripture is the one in which Jesus showed that with faith we could calm the sea. We need to meditate on such situations and why they are so telling. A woman in Florida named Tess Rohmann lives where two huge hurricanes made landfall during 2004 and explained how she placed a sign on her home that said, *"As for me and my House, we will serve the Lord."* It had the Christian symbol of a fish on it.

"Our home is on the barrier islands of Brevard County, Indian Harbour Beach to be exact," said Tess. "It was built prior to Hurricane Andrew [far under current building codes], so its construction is wood frame with sprayed stucco. Our windows are the older single glass and as we prepared to evacuate for Hurricane Frances, I looked around and made to decision to walk out with my Bibles, prayer books, a couple of my favorite statues, insurance papers, family photos, and a couple of very special keepsakes. Everything else I turned my back on. For me it was a powerful spiritual exercise. I made the sign of the fish with the words from Joshua and placed it at our front door taped to the inside of the glass."

This was the only thing that Tess and her husband put up on their home! Her husband told her that if it took a hit with winds of up 100 miles per hour, their house could not withstand it, but they did not put up a single piece of plywood.

Frances battered that coast for over 24 hours. It should have been devastating. But when Tess returned, "our home was not only standing but had *no damage* at all, not even a torn screen! My family was amazed."

"A week later we got ready to leave for Hurricane Jeanne. While others had left their plywood in place, I still had my hand-made 'fish sign' taped to the front door. In the hotel that night my boys asked me to make a sign for our window.

"Well," she continues, "Jeanne hit with such force — there was so much destruction in our area — that we prayed all night and watched news updates in horror. We returned home on Monday and as we crossed the causeway on the way into town, the devastation was very evident. We turned onto our street and saw our neighbor's home with the sides torn off. But when we pulled up to our home, there it stood, with the small crudely handmade sign taped to the glass at the front door. We had absolutely no damage, not even a drop of water inside — not a tear in our screen — although there were many tree branches piled against the screens. *No damage at all* – nothing — and we even had electricity!"

When Mount Etna erupted in 2002 (threatening a complex of buildings), the local archbishop climbed the mountain with forestry officials and offered a benediction.

Experts later admitted that "against all the odds" the river of fire stopped just yards from a complex of buildings, veering off course in what a headline called "Divine Intervention."

In Colchester, Connecticut, a statue survived even though the church was destroyed in an explosion that scattered debris over a huge area.

Chapter 8

Attach yourself to God

There is a shield of power, an energy transcending all known forces, that attaches itself to those who attach themselves to the Lord. Grace surrounds that which is of God. When God wants something for you, you get it. And He watches out for you. I remember the account of a woman who had a near-death brush and how, when she returned, with a heightened sense of perception, she caught sight of evil spirits trying to approach her. "Suddenly, a huge dome of light, almost like glass, fell over me, and the creatures lunged forward, seeming to recognize its threat to them," she recalled. "The dome protected me as they frantically flailed at it and tried to climb on it to get a better vantage point. But the dome was too high to climb on, and they became frustrated."

I think the most astonishing example of such protection was at the original "ground zero." I'm speaking of Hiroshima, where on August 6, 1945, a ten-kiloton atomic bomb was exploded over that Japanese city and there was damage like never seen before on earth. About 140,000 instantly died from the blast or by the end of the year from the effects of radiation. There was a flash of light like a gigantic welder's torch, then fiery tornadic wind. According to one study, the zone of vaporization extended a quarter of a mile from the epicenter. Total destruction ranged for half a mile.

Keep these numbers in mind, because just eight blocks from ground zero, or just over half a mile, was a home with a little conjoined church, tended to by eight Jesuit missionaries. The missionaries were dedicated to daily prayer, especially the Rosary, and had just finished morning Mass when there was the bright flash of light. "Suddenly, a terrific explosion filled the air with one bursting thunderstroke," recalled one of the priests, Father Hubert Schiffer. "An invisible force lifted me from the chair, hurled me through the air, shook me, battered me, and whirled me around and around like a leaf in a gust of autumn wind."

By all measures, Father Schiffer should have died right there. He was in a zone of tremendous mayhem. But he and his seven colleagues survived despite the total devastation around them. Later, scientists studied the seemingly inexplicable circumstances, interviewing the priests on more than 200 occasions. They never did come up with an answer. The priests did not sicken in any way that could be attributed to radiation, and their home still stood, though virtually nothing else did. The remaining area was riddled with fires that stretched out to the final edge at a little over three miles in diameter – far beyond their location.

In fact, at two and a half miles, everything flammable had burned.

"There are no physical laws to explain why the Jesuits were untouched in the Hiroshima air blast," one scientist stated. "There is no other actual or test data where a structure such as this was not totally destroyed at this standoff distance by an atomic weapon. All who were at this range from the epicenter should have received enough radiation to be dead within at most a matter of minutes."

That is the actual definition of a miracle: something that appears to deviate from natural laws. How do we bring one on? How do we seek for ourselves that "shield"?

We can pray: "Please surround me with a perimeter of Your Love and Protection throughout the day today a hundred yards in all directions, dear Lord. Render any demons that are there, or should try to come, deaf, dumb, and blind. Strip them of all weapons, illusions, armor, power, and authority. Disable them from communicating or interacting in any way. Bind, sever, and separate them sending them directly to the foot of Your Cross without manifestation or harm. May Your Precious Blood cover me, the Holy Spirit fill me, Mary's mantle surround me, the Holy Angels and Saints guard and protect me from all unfortunate events. Protect me from fire, theft, flood, storms, ailments, accidents of every sort, and all untoward things. I ask all this in your Name Lord Jesus. I thank you. I praise you. I love you. Amen. Alleluia."

Prayer that is specific is important, and it's crucial to pray such prayers from the heart, not just as rote recitations (as too many do). Most important is to pray that we are in conformance with His "perfect will." We must be living the way He wants us to live.

With that conformity comes the bubble of protection. His Will *is* the protection. It is the power of every miracle.

The more we go along with His plan for us, the more miraculous is the power around us because God is around us. He helps us do His bidding. Live according to what God has in mind for you, as did those missionary priests, and the larger the wonders will grow, as will the protection.

If we're in perfect conformance with God, not even the sky is the limit; a miracle is larger than an atom bomb, as Father Schiffer showed.

But first we have to discern His Mind, and there is no process as tricky as discernment. To attach ourselves to God we must know where He is! Many times in life, we find that there are too many facts to distill into a decision. Knowing this limitation is important. "When He, the Spirit of Truth, comes, He will guide you into all the truth," says *John* 16:13. So pray to Him.

Doing anything else, praying for something against His Will, is at best a waste of time, however good it may seem on the surface. We may get what we want, but things don't quite turn out and tension – even tragedies — come along with it. Pray to know what God wants from you. Do what they call "surrender." Give yourself to God. It's when we maintain the urge to control our destinies – to shape them as *we* want to shape them, as we want to create them — that we stymie miracles. God is in charge of that! Oh, we may do okay. We may even get rich. Efforts often lead to financial reward. There are mechanics in the world that allow for that.

But we won't be happy. Without living in God's Plan, we cannot find peace of mind because we sense a lack of protection. Praying for God's Will to be revealed is a crucial prayer that should precede every other prayer and will in fact lead us to knowing what to pray next.

The Holy Spirit even likes to do our praying for us. His Plan may be far "smaller" than you thought. Maybe He "only" wants you to be good. In fact you can be sure of that. What you do is not nearly as important, to the God of wonders, as how you do it. Maybe His Plan is for you to help a certain person, or simply orient and purify your family. No small task! It can be done only through prayer. Start with that prayer – from the heart – for His Will and Protection.

Then start out small. Pray for the little things. Pray that your kids clean up their rooms. Pray that you get a good night's sleep. Pray until what you need happens, until you are attached and protected. Pray that what you're cooking or working at or striving for turns out the way God wants it to turn out. Tend to the details.

The Lord is a God of details (look at the fine etchings in the innermost feathers of a bird) and is aware of everything, no matter its size.

So pray for every detail and watch how God tends to those details.

Go through a situation in which you need His help and pray for every nuance.

With repeated prayer the details will fall into place and in time do so in a way that is miraculous.

Chapter 9

Wait for the sense of peace

Be diligent. Be persistent. Tend to details. Do His Will. And don't just toss up a quick prayer. Pray like you mean it, which means putting emotion behind it. Clean the slate; wait very patiently; and handle all with humility, reconciliation, and love.

If you love, you will not fear because God is love and He is around you. This brings us to another important element: enthusiasm.

Be enthusiastic. Just as persistence indicates a deeper level of faith, so does enthusiasm. Be enthusiastic about prayer, about God, and about what you expect. To be enthusiastic is to live out the meaning of the word, for enthusiasm comes from two Greek words, *en* and *theos,* meaning, to be in God. There is no limit to what we can accomplish in His power. When we are not afraid of failure, but trust in the Lord, and persist, we always find ourselves with 12 baskets left over.

Enthusiasm is the energy that transcends darkness.

You may be tested for a "season" (on occasion, the Lord will hold back grace), but if you keep to it, are enthusiastic, and *persevere*, matters will fall into place.

The more you pray, the more results you will see, and the more your faith will grow, which unlocks the miracles that God has in store for you. Did you know that God has a storehouse of wonders he would like to give to you? When we die we'll be shown this "storehouse" and be disappointed we didn't attain more of what is in it.

How do we secure what God has earmarked for us, and especially how do we obtain what we need to fulfill our missions?

We pray and let the Holy Spirit inspire us. He does so consciously and through our subconscious. Prayer is the language of miracles, and the more we do it, the more we click into the rhythm of miracles. Reading the Bible aloud, reciting the Scriptural Rosary, and attending Mass are among the most effective for me. Most potent are prayers that go directly to Jesus. Asking Christ to be your Savior, and then speaking with Him as if He were right there, establishing a personal relationship, will take you to a new level.

Repetitious prayers, especially ones said when we're paying close attention to the words, count for much, in the way that God counts any acknowledgement; they open doors, even when they are said a bit absently; God takes note of such prayers because they indicate that at least we have Him on our minds! Pray in any way you are comfortable.

But spontaneous prayer from deep within is most effective. You must go to Christ. You have to treat Him as a friend. He doesn't wish any distance from you. If it is a set prayer, pay attention to the words. Pray as slowly as you can. Envision the Lord. Envision the saints around you. Project yourself to God. Feel the angels.

Let it all hang out. Christ wants you to spill your troubles to Him in more detail than you relate even to your spouse. Involve Him in every word, decision, and struggle, pleading for the knowledge to know His Will. The Lord helps every person on earth, but those who pray open the door to that storehouse.

Conduct a mental dialogue with Jesus. "Rejoice always; pray without ceasing; in everything give thanks; for this is God's will for you in Christ Jesus," says *1 Thessalonians* 5:16-18 — and to do this requires that we think of God in all we do. He wants to be a part of all, and when we consult Him, with eyes upward, in a way that is constant, we are involving Him in every aspect of our lives and finding the rhythm of His blessings.

We can pray everywhere, in the kitchen, in the car, or even while we are shopping, and we are fulfilled when we end up cooking with an extra delicious touch or buying just the right gift or getting to where we need to go on time. When my wife went to decorate our children's rooms, she prayed over the details and it came together beautifully and inexpensively and in a way that she could not have organized herself. The same has occurred when we have gone on trips.

We must go to God for everything, invoking Him in every thought and activity. This makes us partners with Him. How do we tell if we're partners? We know when something is right because the Holy Spirit *grants* us the knowing, and this provides serenity. Instead of allowing in anxiety, instead of tossing and turning, we need to take a deep breath, relax, and pray through Jesus.

Yearning for God, seeing Him in everything, and thanking Him at every juncture creates an open channel.

Gee, Father, please help me, I really have to make this decision... or settle this issue...or get this job...

Talk to Him as you would a buddy, and wait for Him to prompt you; He will do so with the sense of peace.

Chapter 10

Don't force things

A feeling of uneasiness, second-guessing, and butting one's head against the wall is a clear sign of the unmiraculous.

Only when we calm ourselves and delve into prayer do matters clarify (underscore the word "clarify"), and no decision should be made without such clarification.

When there is clarity, which accompanies peace, the Holy Spirit, the miraculous, is with us.

The opposite is true when we agonize.

Turning things over in your mind will wear you out and muddy the issue. *Should I go out with him? Is that job really what I want? Is that the place I should move to?* When we repeat these questions, to obsession, agonizing, we are counter-miraculous.

Often there are so many variables in making a decision that it's impossible to line them all up, analyze each one, and make the right decision. Only God can do that because only He can know all the variables and put them in proper perspective.

When we try, when we put *ourselves* in charge, we agonize.

You may be going through such a decision right now. Just remember that it does no good to burn a hole in it. Don't try to be what God did not intend you to be. Forget the standards of the "world." Our greatest inhibitor is worldliness!

The Lord wants us to lay it in His lap, to *really* go to Him, to send it with the stamp of our hearts on it. When we do, Heaven rushes to help. In New York was the mother of a toddler who was run over by the family's SUV. The father was driving. He backed over his son's head. Imagine the distress! Yet the boy made a miraculous recovery. "At first we didn't even know if he was going to live," said the mom. "Now he's walking up and down the halls. He's talking. He's reading. All I did was give it to God and pray," she told a newspaper.

Surround it with prayer. Give it to God. Do things for the benefit of others. When prayers are answered, spend time thanking the Lord. Ideally, we should spend as much time in *thanks* as in *request*. This works wonders.

Years ago I got an offer to do a book for one of the nation's largest publishers and the offer was significantly more than my agent and I expected. I sat down and thanked God by reading the entire Book of Psalms in one very long sitting (even though it was an abbreviated Bible). It's a wonderful way of thanking Him, and the next day my agent called with more stunning news: the publisher wanted to make sure we didn't go to another firm and increased the advance by half.

God loves when we are grateful. During thanksgiving we are expressing love for Him. We are close to Him. We are brought into His Plan. When we thank God, we are stepping out of ourselves and into His power.

That makes a world – a universe – of difference. Miracles are often instant and big when we go to Him and don't force things. Too often, we get an idea and push for it despite gut feelings. We shouldn't do that. We should respect the intuition that God gave to us. Get in touch with your deepest inclinations. Those are your signposts. There you will find His still, small voice (*1 Kings* 19:11-18). If we're honest, we know there are countless times when we sense that the Lord may want something but forge ahead with what we want. We convince ourselves that something is right when in our hearts we know that it *isn't* right, and in this way we force matters to fit when they don't. Most failures are the result of jamming our ideas into a situation that requires a different course of action, and the fruit of forcing anything is breakage.

We break things. Sometimes, it is even disaster. Take a key that does not go with a lock and it won't open the door. The fruit of forcing something is blockage.

True, there are also times when we're blocked because we're doing the right thing and it is the enemy blocking us. But most of the time we are *wasting* our time when we push one way despite signs pointing in the other direction. How do we tell the right course? How do we discern the "signs"? A feeling of tranquility is a benchmark. When something is "right" for us, when it fits in God's Plan, we feel at peace. God comes closer and there is a feeling of well-being. There is fullness. We feel right about it. This is God communicating, and He is ready to guide us in any situation. Try praying to the Holy Spirit even when you go shopping and in some way the Lord will direct you (especially if you are buying for someone else).

This feeling of peace usually is accompanied by the lifting of our spiritual blinders. We begin to see the spiritual reasons for all that occurs around us. It's like stepping backstage, and it comes in a special way through fasting, deep prayer, and the sacraments. During Communion — which means communication — Christ often communicates what He expects from us. The Lord wants us to be humble, accomplish our duties according to our stations in life, and be open to His inspiration. Every inspiration, every good thought, is a miracle. They let you know or "feel" which decisions are right and which are wrong, according to your purpose in life. A decision that's not in God's Will oppresses, binds, worries, and causes you to second guess. Always be on the lookout for uneasiness. Other hallmarks are anxiety, vacillation, and confusion, which signify that for some reason the Lord is distant. As soon as you sense confusion, you should stop deciding whatever you're deciding and go to the Lord until the confusion lifts.

If you start by doing that, you'll begin to invoke God on a more frequent basis. He'll become more involved, and the involvement of God is the involvement of the supernatural.

"There are two ways to live your life," goes the saying. "One is as though nothing is a miracle. The other is as though everything is a miracle."

Choose the latter. See God everywhere. Hear Him. Decide with Him. The results will be astonishing.

How do we tell if we have made a correct decision? If we look deeply into our lives, we'll find that the right decisions have tended toward our deepest life purpose. Find your purpose and don't expect it to be grandiose. God doesn't want for you to do big things to glorify yourself, but to seek big things in "small" acts, and to fulfill His designs without trumping yourself up. He doesn't want you to reach beyond your station. A station in life is our role in life, whether an engineer or a housewife. Remember that there are great spirits with special missions at all levels of society and in every station. Great souls are placed at every "station of life." God has put everyone in spots where they can benefit others. He has placed us to minister. He has positioned us to fight the spiritual war on all levels — whether in a board room or on a construction site. Our mission in life is to teach and test each other in the way of love. You may have more opportunity to touch others as a cleaning woman than a stockbroker. Who then has the greater mission? It's when we try to climb out of our assignment that we cause ourselves discontent.

Seek God. Strive for the big in the little. The Lord is revealed in what is small, and such is an ingredient of balance: to know who we are, Who we need, and what we need to accomplish. Often the one who seeks for much does not receive even the little. The Lord searches for our goodness.

Goodness is something that benefits others as well as ourselves and in doing so brings our actions into alignment with His Plan.

It is when we are cooperating with His Plan that He grants a full blessing. Alignment is very important. We note that Christ gave the "cup" to the Father and the result was the greatest miracle in history: resurrection. Real grace requires the right decision and the right decision is almost always something that is done for an unselfish reason and benefits others.

Back in my days as a reporter I became involved in the investigation of a situation called Love Canal, in which toxic chemicals were threatening a community. The reports soon led to formation of citizen activists and helped propel major governmental action. While getting a "scoop" was always important, the main motive was to help the people. My job became a vehicle to assist others, and I was astonished at the results: for years after, God blessed my work and I went from being a local reporter in a small city to writing national magazine articles, speaking on the college lecture circuit, and landing a major book contract as a 27-year-old writer in an excellent part of Manhattan.

I yielded, and the Lord fit me into His Plan in ways I would not dared to have imagined.

Other times, I've seen the opposite when I have sought my own interest.

There was blockage. There was no peace. There was a lack of clarity.

We may succeed with selfish ambition to a point and even make a lot of money (the world takes care of the worldly); but when the main motive is our own benefit, there is never fulfillment. The course that grants us happiness is His course; it may take us years or even decades to see it, but it's true: Working toward the common good, we are brought to a higher vision while blind ambition leads to a blind alley.

Chapter 11

Rise out of self

If you want to be blind, be selfish. See everything from your viewpoint and only your viewpoint. Make yourself the god of your own world. In no time your vision will cloud and you'll find that there are no stars in your part of the cosmos.

There are also no miracles. When we are selfish, we have trouble seeing the spiritual forces that swirl around us.

Each act of selfishness causes a little blot and the blots add up to a patch of blackness.

If you want to check to see if you are selfish, question the motive of everything you desire and examine everything that offends you.

Why were you offended? What part of you did it engage? Did it "hurt your pride," or challenge your subtle viewpoint of superiority?

Ask the Holy Spirit to reveal your true inner life and if there is too much "self," purge it. Pray until it is gone. Rise above it.

To rise means to reorient, and the archaic definition of "reorient" is "resurrection."

When we reorient toward unselfishness, we grow more like Christ.

Step out of your "self" like you would step out of dirty clothes and a new reality will rise around you.

How else do we know if there is "self"? From it come impatience, anger, insult, depression, phobias, grudges, and retributions. Who do you dislike, and why? What engages the negative side of you?

We must know this because the negative will block you, quash the spirit, and is anti-miraculous.

There is no way for a person who is selfish to encounter true miracles – only the miracles of the world, which are eaten, in the end, by the worm, or rust in the mist of dawn (see *Jonah* 4:7).

The opposite is true when we are selfless and we know we are selfless, when we think of everything from the perspective of others, when we get the greatest joy out of giving, when we easily forgive, and when depriving ourselves doesn't lead to an emotional crisis. An example is a woman in California whose mission is to bury the little babies that have been abandoned. She does so on a little plot near the town of Calimesa – deceased infants. She was entirely unselfish, serving God in a real need, and it caused a miracle. There were always the calls informing her of another newborn at the morgue, but in 2004 she got a different call, this one informing her that she had won $27 million in the California lottery – which she immediately announced would go to furthering her work.

Her unselfishness had lubricated a huge miracle.

Those with similar funds hurt themselves if they don't use it to make miracles for others.

The less self there is, the more there is God, Who wants you in His universe, not your own. Our sun must be His Son.

Live for others and learn to make sacrifices. Pray for everyone you encounter (especially those you dislike) and offer all you do to the Lord. Love especially in circumstances in which it is most difficult to love. Note how many "hurts" are caused solely because you have not rid yourself *of* self.

Our starting point in everything has to be the desire of God, followed by consideration for what best serves fellow humans. Envision yourself stepping out of your self and view yourself as one of many. Don't take the "I" approach, but the "we" approach. Look upon everything as for God. Let Him to be center of gravity. Step out of the "self" and it will lead us to an attitude of sacrifice – which brings us into critical communion with the Lord.

Chapter 12

'Live in the Voice of God'

When we do that, when we live for Him, when we sacrifice, and when we repent, God often responds with a miracle. A blunder is followed by a wonder. Persist, strive to help others, do so with enthusiasm, with fearlessness. Now you are headed for the deep areas of faith and contact with the God of miracles.

Simply put, surrender.

"Trust in the Lord with all your heart and lean not on your own understanding," says *Psalms* 3:5-6. "In all your ways acknowledge Him, and He will make your paths straight."

In other words, He will communicate if you let go and go with His flow. The God of miracles is a God Who talks and will direct you. He spoke the world into existence. He spoke and the Word was made flesh. Any good thought we have is derived from Him. All the brilliant ideas, all the innovations that lead to good, all the ways we have evolved in a positive fashion, were all whispered to us, originating in the Spirit. His communication with us is basically the soft touch of direction, the sensation of "feeling right."

Usually He does so in a fashion that is exquisitely subtle – so subtle that it's hard to distinguish from your own thoughts. He plants ideas, and we are free to choose or reject them.

They are a spontaneous "knowing"; they are "promptings" or hunches.

God infuses us with His knowledge; aside from life itself, aside from our very consciousness, aside from the very way He holds things together, it is His most common miracle.

I once heard a "voice" that saved me from a fire, and had a premonition of being in a smoke-filled home the week before it happened. He caused that because He loves us. His Voice has also saved you – has led you not to go somewhere at a certain time, has kept you out of harm's way, has changed your routine when you could have been in an accident — more times than you know.

A nurse wrote to me about how the father of a newborn called the nursery at two a.m. one night and urged them, out of nowhere, to check his baby. "I assured him the baby was fine, but that I would check," she recalled. "When I went to the bassinette, the baby was blue and having problems due to vomiting."

Mainly God speaks to us in thoughts (instead of words), through events, and through other people. He'll give us a sudden and intense interest in something He wants us to do or in something that would be good for us. They call it an "infusion" (or inspiration) and I'll give you another example. Years ago I got on the scale for the first time in a decade and was startled to see that I weighed 202 pounds. That was surprising because I'd always viewed myself as thin – weighing 135 pounds when I graduated from college.

Yet now, in my forties, I was fat. What I saw on the scale shocked and astonished me.

Frustrated, immediately I sat on my bed, prayed to the Holy Spirit, and ideas that were not my own came cascading into my head. Immediately I felt "told" to completely eliminate soda and salt (I never thought about the use of salt), to cut down on lunch, and to drink as much water as I could – all foreign ideas to me! The cutting out of salt worked wonders. I heeded what I was "told" and within two months was down to 165 (and am praying to stay there).

There are hunches. There are "gut feelings." Let me give you a better example — the account of a woman in Greenwood, Indiana. Her name is Joy English, and she had lost her 27-year-old son in a hit-and-run. The night before Thanksgiving in 2004, she was driving to a store to buy flowers for his grave when she felt "guided" to turn into a mobile home park a few miles from her home.

"I went the long way ... and as I was driving I had this urgent prompting to pull over — pull over now!" she said, explaining that she was thinking of her son and crying as she listened to Christmas music — when she did as she was "told" and saw a van that matched the description of the one that hit her son. She said she felt she had "no control" over her car as she drove into that trailer park and it was there that she saw the van, which ended up bearing tell-tale matches with debris left at the scene, where her son had been killed as he rode a bike.

She wrote down the van's license plate number, called the police, and soon after, a call from an official at the Marion County sheriff's department confirmed her hunch.

"You found your son's killer," the deputy told Joy, who said the experience made her "know that God is truly with us in our mourning, sorrow and trials," that He "is truly with you."

As indeed He is, every moment. Most of the time, He is quiet, but He can use any means to communicate with us. He has spoken by way of hand-writing on the wall (*Daniel* 5:1-30) and through a sonorous voice (as when He told John the Baptist about Jesus). According to Balaam, he once spoke through the mouth of a donkey (*Numbers* 22:21-33)! Usually, His interactions are the very definition of "subtlety," occurring through normal means that in reality are little miracles. Such occur when we are contemplating an issue and that very day, at Mass, or while reading the Bible, something is read that perfectly answers the question.

How many times have you picked up a book or newspaper and had a solution hit you between the eyes?

There is a continual interplay with God and He is always involved with us. Every decision, every cast of the lots, says *Proverbs* 16:33, "is from the Lord." He speaks to us in the flow of events. Often something that happens is a miniature preview of what could occur, positive or negative. He gives us those feelings of comfort. When it is right for you, it fits like an old shoe. The opposite is true of the wrong decision, which will rub against you. Any anxiousness is a signal. If in doubt, leave it out. There are "little" ways that He guides us.

When God does speak loudly, it's unforgettable, and every word – every syllable — counts. At Assisi in Italy I once heard the words, *"Communicate with confidence."* Those three words changed my entire career as an author. Others report even more overt experiences. There is June Klins. She was praying for her in-laws, both of whom committed suicide (due to horrendous physical pain), and she desperately wanted to know if they were okay (if, upon death, they had avoided hell).

The sign June asked for was two white roses, and one day, after a long series of Masses for them, she was returning from their graves when she saw a dozen white roses were on her doorstep, along with a toy dog.

The stuffed animal was identical to a dog her father-in-law once owned!

Her relief was immeasurable. As it turns out, the roses had been sent by a friend who didn't know about her request for a sign but had simply awoken the night before and heard a voice say, *"Get June white roses"*!

The Lord may also send images.

"I had a beautiful experience of losing the rosary that I had as a postulant some forty years ago," recalls Sheila Torres. "I was driving the car and inwardly I asked myself, 'I wonder where that rosary is.' Instantly in my thoughts I 'saw' a picture of a purse up in the closet and that it was in the zipper pocket of that purse. When I got home, I looked, and there it was!"

Often in prayer something or someone "pops" into our heads and our thinking clarifies. Heed those images. It could be something you have to watch or someone you need to pray for. It's hard to imagine a more urgent case than what faced Jon Stockton, a kayaker who was on vacation in Hawaii and was swept out to sea – at some points during a five-day ordeal, more than eighty miles from the big island. One can only imagine his anxiety and fatigue! Finally he gave it all to God. "I just said, 'Lord, my arms are just like wet noodles of spaghetti,'" he recounted. "There's no strength in them at all. They're sore. They're tired,' and I just started saying, 'Lord, what do I do?' I felt like the Lord said, *'Paddle and use your cell phone.'"*

Jon was so far out at sea that he had assumed that his phone would not work, but when he pulled it out of his waterproof bag and tried, it worked long enough for him to dial 911 and get an emergency operator — who took down minimal directions but just enough before the connection was lost. Soon he was rescued by a plane.

When God does speak in actual words, they usually come in a way that's unexpected. They are not something we expect, conjure, or strain to hear. As St. Teresa of Avila taught, God speaks in "thoughts" that cost us no expenditure of energy. Every word counts – there is an economy of language — and each word is indelible.

Of course, we have to discern such voices. The devil also speaks, and his is the louder and more insistent voice. Scripture tells us to test the spirits. Thus, there can be great danger in overly focusing on voices.

Usually, God's advice comes through the intuition – in the process of thinking — and the miraculous life is the one that recognizes His Word in the normal flow of things.

We receive that in proportion to how much we have surrendered.

"Speak, Lord, for Your servant is listening," was Eli's advice (*1 Samuel* 3:9). A mystic from Ecuador once put it in an interesting way when she said that we must live "in the Will and Voice of God."

Nothing is more important.

Living in the Voice of God is not so much watching for extraordinary signs as living with a realization that everything around you has a spiritual component. In *Genesis* it says that the Lord spoke and we were created and so His Words are the very essence of life, which is one constant series of miracles. You can prove this by putting your hand in front of your face, sticking out one of your fingers, and bending it. You have just witnessed several miracles. The spirit has conveyed information to the body through the brain and created three near-instantaneous reactions.

I use the word "miracle" because a miracle is any interaction between the physical and the spiritual. We live in a sea of energy that flows from the Holy Spirit and that power permeates everything. When we recognize this all-encompassing force, the concept of miracles and His communication is easy. Remember the saying, "all of the brain is in the mind, but not all of the mind is in the brain"? That's another way of putting it: the mind or spirit instills an idea into the neurons of the brain, where they are routed to various parts of the body.

It is the *spirit* (not the lucky forces of nature) that holds everything together and prevents chaos. If not for God, everything would quickly fall into chaos. Throughout the universe is a natural inclination toward "entropy," which means that something left alone will deteriorate. This we know from simply looking at our yards. If we don't cut the grass for a couple weeks, or don't treat wood, or don't protect metal from rain, what happens to it? And what happens to the body when the spirit leaves it?

The Lord Who speaks to us organizes us and enlivens the body. We know there is an intelligent component of the universe – and as I said a force behind everything — by the simple fact that slight differences in countless aspects of the cosmos would each quash human existence, if left alone. As scientists have pointed out, many of the most basic features of the universe, such as electromagnetism, gravity, and the forces that keep atomic nuclei together, are so finely tuned that if but *one* were slightly different, life as we know it would not be possible.

A British philosophy professor who had been a leading champion of atheism for more than a half-century changed his mind and now believes in God, he recently said, because a super-intelligence is the only good explanation for the origin of life and the complexity of nature. He pointed out that the investigation of DNA "has shown, by the almost unbelievable complexity of the arrangements which are needed to produce life, that intelligence must have been involved."

It is a caring God Who did that and Who is so wondrously creative that everyone has unique faces as well as unique fingerprints.

Chapter 13

Don't limit yourself

Thus do we see that without God, without an interaction with Him, there is decay, not "evolution."

Everything that grows and reproduces (instead of deteriorating) is a miracle.

Just as subatomic particles are kept together, so are events in our lives.

God orchestrates our existence just as He orchestrates the forces in outer space. When we pray about even the smallest details, everything about us also "holds together." We are on the way to cohesion. Breakfast is perfect, the car starts right up, and people are unusually pleasant to us.

Does that mean praying about every detail will make everything smooth every time we do so? There are trials. Often, one day is excellent and the next is the opposite.

But give it a chance – pray for every little thing before you're even out of bed, every detail you can think of — and then keep your mind on God the rest of the day. Ask Him to direct your every move. Go through all you need, every item, and make your requests.

"Ask and you will receive," says Scripture (*John* 16:24) – and often we simply forget to do that.

Don't limit yourself. Pray slowly; focus on each word; slow prayers pierce the clouds.

God loves our requests and He loves to bless.

Two roses?

How about, as with June, a dozen?

But we have to ask and all of us should do that every day. While it's true that God knows what we need before we request it, He likes to hear it from us. It opens a channel. When we feel down, when we have problems and needs, we must pray with the knowing that if it's right for us (if it's correct in the larger picture only He can see), He will grant it. If it is His Will, or at least something that is not against His Will, matters will "click."

When that happens He is really speaking to us! We know such is true when there is no strain and events unfold like the leaves of a plant — organically. Sometimes it's beneficial to note these occurrences in a diary, because the more we notice them, the more our faith grows, the more we surrender, the more future prayers are answered.

Surrender means to yield to a higher power.

Whose power is more effective, yours or His?

Once we view life in such a context – noting all the times that God has answered a prayer — we are living a life of miracles. Just keep in mind that everything is in God's Providence — when we *bring* it into His Providence.

We could call that "acknowledgement." We acknowledge His role in everything. We listen for Him. We do as He prompts. This takes us from basic faith to the level of persistence, which deepens into surrender and causes effects for which we are eternally grateful.

See how it all dovetails? Surrender involves not only faith but also humility and love.

That brings us to appreciation, which is extremely powerful in drawing down the God of miracles – Who is humble but wants to be appreciated; in this way does He enjoy our love.

The more directly we show our gratitude, the more powerfully He intervenes.

Of course, thanking God should not be done for that reason. Our main motive must be affection for Him. *When He holds back His response,* it is often to test our motives, so it is always important to examine our motivation. Are our lives oriented toward God? Are we functioning at the station in life He assigned to us? Have we surrendered? Are we appreciative? Are we living for Him or ourselves?

Those are crucial questions, for God has no trouble discerning motives and doesn't respond to the wrong ones.

Ungratefulness blocks grace because it's an indication that we think *we* brought the good upon ourselves or think we deserve whatever it is we have received, that we "had it coming," when really we deserve nothing.

The Lord wants to know if we are loyal and have surrendered and this is seen when we are appreciative. "O give thanks to the Lord, call upon His name," says *1 Chronicles* 16:8. "Save us, O God of our salvation, and gather us and deliver us from the nations, to give thanks to Your Holy Name."

"I will give thanks to the Lord with all my heart; I will tell of all Your wonders," says *Psalms* 26:7 "I will praise the Name of God with song, and magnify Him with thanksgiving."

Hover over the word "wonders":

By my count it's used more than sixty times in the Bible and is what "attested" to the supernatural nature of Jesus.

Hover too over the verb "magnify":

The more grateful we are, the larger God looms.

Thank Him for your life, your friends, your children, your spouse, your parents, home, food, work, everything in life, every day, and through the day, and the miracles will grow. Why is thanksgiving so powerful? It is a verbalization of faith. "Always giving thanks," says *Ephesians* 5:20, "for all things in the name of our Lord Jesus Christ to God, even the Father"!

Praise and thanks to God throughout the day make it a blessed day even if it doesn't happen to be an *easy* one.

Fruit will come of it. Note that *Ephesians* goes on to tell us that thankfulness keeps away the "fiery darts" of the enemy.

If we could see with spiritual eyes, we would see the proximity to danger, how it is only the thin wall of our homes that separates us from the elements – in many areas, from scorpions, from venomous snakes – and how inside our homes are swarming with organisms that could cause disease but against which we are protected by His bubble.

Can you imagine how many times you could have been injured, that you could have been in an accident, that you could have taken ill, that you could have run out of money, that you could have lost or missed or broken something if not for the ever-watchful Heart of Jesus?

Think about it: God is responsible for our very existence; it would take an infinity of Thanksgivings to thank Him just for that.

The simple words of thanks bring a mother lode of blessings because they put us in contact with God at a more intense level. Each day, or at least every week, we need to meditate on all we have been both spared and given. If we think long enough, the list is endless.

After thanking comes *orderliness,* because when we are orderly, we are flowing with Him.

To be orderly is to take care of ourselves, our surroundings, and especially what God has given us. In a way, *orderliness is a sign of gratitude.* It's not something we think about very often (at least not in the context of religion) but God is the Lord of orderliness, which means that He wants us to be disciplined. He wants self-control.

"The corrections of discipline are the way to life," says *Proverbs* 6:23.

The more orderly we are, the cleaner, brighter that we appear, and cleanliness is next to Godliness.

Recall how patiently Christ waited for His public ministry, steadfastly worked toward the end of His mission, disciplined His words, and extensively fasted – which is a hallmark of self-control. In many, many aspects of life, discipline is the key to happiness.

When we fast we are putting things in order, and I have seen great miracles performed with it. This is one of the more surprising spiritual rules: that with prayer and fasting we can even suspend the laws of nature.

God comes rushing to our sides when we fast because we are openly declaring an independence from the flesh, demonstrating a union with Christ, and forging spiritual orderliness. To fast is to transcend the "world." To fast is to put the spiritual first. It brings us health. It brings us attractiveness. It brings us to prayer. It brings us income. It also purges the spirit. When we overcome temptation, we move beyond our bodies to the spiritual, wherein resides the miraculous. Our spirits are given greater reign and are more able to function at a transcendental level when we discipline ourselves.

When God sees that we have the mark of orderliness, He's freer to trust us with more gifts. If you meditate on it, you will find that it solves most major problems. To regulate oneself is to "hold fast," to use verbiage from *Deuteronomy,* and when we despise ourselves, we are holding fast onto God instead of things of this world. Nothing distances you more from God than grasping onto the material, including food, which is why gluttony is considered a capital sin (and in our time is rampant).

When we are disciplined, it gives us a direct line to God. It tells Him that we're serious. It rebukes the devil, whose mission is to tempt. We find protection.

Fast in whatever way you can, but deny yourself of something that shows God you can thrust yourself above the carnal. To fast means to be stead*fast*, tenacious, and thankful, as in the Book of Psalms, where we are constantly reminded of praise, thankfulness, and God's wonders.

Chapter 14

Place on your lips the words,
'thank you, Jesus'

It all dovetails and we have to remember that gratitude also means to stop complaining. An excellent fast is to stop being *negative*.

Nothing quashes the miraculous like negativity. Why?

Negativity is a lack of gratefulness and that ingratitude separates us from God.

To be negative is to detract, to criticize, to look for the bad. It is a lack of love. In mathematics it's symbolized by the "minus" sign, and we see a clue right there. It is less than nothing, below zero; the minus sign is an incomplete symbol whereas the "plus" sign is complete (and forms a cross).

The dictionary tells us that negativity diminishes the positive.

When we're involved in negativity, it reduces the "plus signs" or blessings that God has earmarked for us. God is positive and (like cables between car batteries) we have to be positive to connect to Him.

When it comes to miracles, negativity is a black hole. That's because when we're negative we're taking away from God's plan instead of adding to it (which is our mission). *God doesn't reward us when we are stepping backward.* And negativity is a slippery slope. One negativity leads to others. They are a spiritual virus. Everyone has seen a photographic negative, which is the reverse of a color picture just as negativity is the reverse of the positive. Note that those pictured in a negative are surrounded by darkness!

This happens to us: when we fall into a negative frame of mind, the distance from God allows in darkness.

What about when someone is wrong? What about when we're critical but correct? There are right ways of approaching it, and ways that are not. When a problem is pointed out with love, it's a correction. That's positive. When there is no love, it's an exercise in "unlove." We can be right in our criticism — accurate as to the facts — and still hurt ourselves if we are acting out of anger.

If there are no miracles in your life, pray to the Holy Spirit to search your soul for anger. Once purged of anger, many things you have prayed for are more likely to receive their answers. Anger blocks because it is the opposite of love and is best represented by criticality and an inability to forgive.

There are times we have to point out faults, even confront another person, but harboring a negative point of view is the entrance to hatred — which is the most powerful of all negative emotions.

As a result, when we take a closer look at those who are negative, we often find a string of unfortunate events.

There will be accidents. There'll be problems at work. There'll be illness. We may ride high for a while, but watch what happens. Negativity often springs from pride, which comes before the fall – sometimes, literally. Negativity brings a cloud of negative "blessings."

At the opposite pole is God, Who surrounds us with light. Sometimes it even glitters. Of the alleged miracles in our time, one of the most baffling is the phenomenon of what looks like glitter, luminous specks that as a sign of God's love appear as if out of nowhere! Is it a real phenomenon? A deception? A hoax? As usual, we have to carefully discern. But God can work mysteriously. In poor parts of South America – where this phenomenon seems to focus – there are churchgoers who claim their decayed teeth were fixed with gold-like fillings that inexplicably appeared after services! In El Salvador it was said that after half an hour of "clap-offering" – wherein God is thanked and praised in a tremendously positive environment — a kind of gold cloud came down upon a stadium.

Can we believe such accounts? In 1998, a missionary in Bethany, Israel, was assisting a handicapped Arab man who could not speak, walk, or use his right hand. She helped him learn to paint abstracts with his good left hand, and he hummed while he did it, listening to Christian music. Later, when the missionary returned to see this man before leaving Israel, she was distraught because he looked so depressed. It turns out that he was no longer painting. His new aides didn't understand how important it was to him and had not kept it up, but she prayed, kept a positive attitude, and the Holy Spirit put everything together — in such a way that before she left, she was able to visit the man and set up his painting, which he did with relish. When the missionary showed his abstracts to friends, they noted that "all three paintings had gold dust sprinkled everywhere and dried into it" — even though there was no gold in the paint.

God was showing how close He is, especially when we help others.

William E. Simon, a former Treasury Secretary and one-time president of the U.S. Olympics Committee – whose very photos seem to radiate the positive — documented the baffling turning to gold of old, inexpensive rosary beads he took on pilgrimage, where he noticed them glittering in the sun.

"That was strange," he recounted. "The chain was just some cheap, dull alloy, yet it suddenly appeared radiant and golden and vibrant and remained so. I wasn't quite sure what to make of it, and upon my return brought the rosary to a jeweler for an appraisal.

"He confirmed that the chain, inexplicably, had turned to solid gold. I can't explain the transformation, either of the rosary or my own life, except as a sign of Divine intervention."

Chapter 15

The prophecy of intuition

As gold shines, so do the faces of those who are positive in the Lord. John Paul II and Mother Teresa had it. Moses' face shone after he encountered the Almighty. There is an aura of brightness when the God of miracles touches us.

Those are overt signs of His presence. In day-to-day living, the signs come in smaller ways but often include another gift: the miracle of prophecy. Those who fix their eyes on God often are led by intuition. They feel things that others cannot feel, and such intuition prevents negativity (or prepares them for a great mission). A man I know in Pennsylvania, who fasts and loves God much, was sitting at his desk and heard the horn of an oncoming train.

Trains passed close to his office half a dozen times a day, but this time, for some reason, he sprang from his desk and felt compelled to run to the street — where he spotted a car sitting on the tracks.

Oblivious (immersed in her headset), the driver didn't hear the throttle – and so just sat there at the crossing.

My friend banged on her window, alerted her to the onrushing locomotive, and saved her life.

He had been given the prophecy of intuition.

The miraculous life functions on intuition that is enhanced by prayer. The more we pray, the more connected we are to the God of miracles. By prayer I don't mean just a few "Praise You Jesuses" or rote phrases (though these never hurt). God seeks to share His knowledge. It takes time. I mean settling down every day and often several times a day and truly seeking Him. It's only a settled and clear state of mind through which the Lord's whisper comes (like the caress of wind).

When we pray, our minds sprout spiritual antennae. A woman from California wrote to describe how her mother was led to suddenly pray for her family at the precise moment that a stranger was trying to abduct her child at Disneyland. The grandmother simply had a "bad feeling" and sat down to recite a Rosary. She heeded her intuition, stopped everything, and prayed. Just then, many miles away, something made her daughter glance at just the right time and catch the abductor trying to spirit away her child!

When we act on such prompts, God gives us more prompts, and then still more, until we're moving firmly (and positively) in the Spirit. We develop what could be called the "momentum of the miraculous." Prayer sharpens the intuition, which also expresses itself in dreams. *God speaks to us through the subconscious and sometimes does so while we're sleeping.* We call it dreaming, and most of it seems like a release of pent-up emotions, as well as an unleashing of the imagination. In a dream state, reality comes in bits and pieces.

In those fragments, however, is often at least a sense of what is to come, and sometimes there is a visual display of foreknowledge or what you might call a "premonition."

A man sees a black-draped casket and a week later a loved one dies; he is thus better prepared for it. Perhaps he sees that loved one waving, as if to say good-bye. A woman dreams of a little boy and then finds out that she's pregnant. She has a boy. Thanks to dreams, Joseph knew to flee to Egypt. "If there is a prophet among you, I the Lord will make Myself known unto him in a vision and will speak unto him in a dream," says *Numbers* 12:6.

I once had a dream in which I saw smoke filling a room next to the one I was sleeping in at my parents' house. It was so vivid that I called the bank the next day to inquire about a safe deposit box for my most valuable papers. In the dream I watched as the smoke rolled in and noticed that there was a layer of clear air near the floor.

The next week there was an electrical fire on that floor and I watched from my room as the smoke did exactly what I had foreseen. Because of the dream, there was no sense of panic; I knew there would be a layer of clear air, and I bent down to breathe below the smoke as I made my way calmly past the flames and escaped.

Does this mean we live according to what we dream? No. Dreams are too erratic. Moreover, God does not usually display the future in such detail. Mostly He sends us hints to prompt us, careful not to infringe on our free will. But there are dramatic exceptions, times when the Lord is both specific and vivid. Before John F. Kennedy was killed, many reported dreams about his assassination, and the same was true of terrorists strikes on September 11. I heard from people who had lucid night-time visions of Arabic men in a plane or folks who woke up because they dreamt of a plane crashing into buildings. In Canada an artist painted a picture of the World Trade Center in which flames were coming from right where the planes would later hit.

Someone sent me a photo of the sun rising between the two towers and emitting horizontal rays that seemed to slice at the same places.

And a gentleman named Paul Wagner wrote about an event that occurred at Palm Springs, California, at sunset of September 10. "My roommate Dan and I decided to drive downtown for dinner," he said. "It was an agreeably warm and clear evening. Driving west in the direction of San Jacinto Mountain, we suddenly observed unusual dark-gray rays of the sun emerging from behind the mountain. Maybe we witnessed the bold rays before, but this time our attention was upon the odd and powerful display in the sky. We returned home from dinner an hour later at about 6:45 p.m. Dan exited the garage and gazed back at the sky. 'Hurry—Look!' he called. In the area where we had observed the powerful dark rays of the sun there was now an immense cloud formation in the shape of two towers, one of which was slightly smaller than the other. The larger of the two appeared three-dimensional, revealing swirling shades of black, gray, and brown. At the base of each cloudlike 'tower' were what appeared to be gray talons that swept down grasping the horizon. Between the two 'towers' was a string of dazzling silver that strangely connected the two. The shocking display was set behind the most exceptional crystal-blue sky. Dan thought it was an ominous and disturbing sign. I agreed, and had never witnessed such a bizarre formation. Yet it seemed more than just a curious cloud: an actual vision. I looked around to see if anyone else was watching, but saw no one. We gazed for a solid five minutes but the formation failed to move or change. Eventually, we went inside only to return about ten minutes later, but the spectacle had transformed into a dark gray formless haze."

Chapter 16

The Lord's inklings prepare us

The God of miracles lends us the miracle of prophecy to prepare us.

Deena Burnett, whose husband Thomas died in that plane above Pennsylvania, told me he had been away from the faith but returned and intensified his religious involvement after their marriage in 1992. As if by intuition, he was preparing for a mission.

Both she and Tom had forebodings.

"After our third daughter was born, I always had this feeling that Tom was not going to live long enough to raise our children, but I never talked to him about this," she recalled. "I shared that thought with my mom right after our third daughter was born. She came into the hospital room and she said, 'Deena, I guess you'll have to have another child so Tom can have his son,' and I said, 'No, mom, God's not going to give us a son.' She said, 'Why?' and I said, 'Because God knows that Tom won't be here to raise the children and I couldn't raise Tom's son alone.'

"My mother asked me what I was talking about, and I don't know why I said that, but I remember feeling an incredible sense of peace, that whatever happened, everything was going to be okay," Deena told me. "It was the week of February 24, 1998, and I also told her then that he was going to be killed in a plane crash. It just came out of my mouth without any thought, and I didn't even think of it after I said it. It was something I was very much at peace with. It was God's plan, preparing me," she added, her voice cracking.

About that time — 1998 — Tom had stopped coming home for lunch. In December the businessman who would die on 9/11 told his wife that the reason he wasn't home was that he was now attending daily Mass. After their marriage, he had become increasingly interested in the Blessed Mother, buying books about the Rosary and expressing a desire to visit shrines in Europe. "He would often bring up his faith in God and never shied away from conversations about it," said Deena of the 38-year-old California executive — who had three daughters, two of them five-year-old twins when he met his fate.

"I was a little bit surprised (by his religious involvement), but I didn't say anything," said Deena. "He said, 'I feel like God is calling me to do something, and I don't know what it is. But I know it's going to have a great impact on a lot of people.' He said, 'The reason I've been going to daily Mass is because I feel like if I can be closer to God, then I'll know what His plan is for me.'"

Deena recounted that from then on, she and Tom spent a great deal of time talking about what that "plan" might be.

"He wasn't sure, but to say he was intuitive is an understatement, and I knew if he felt something was going to happen, I better listen to it and trust him. One of the things we brainstormed about was that he thought it had *something to do with the White House.*"

Because Burnett was an outgoing, charismatic man who was thinking of retiring early from what was already a highly successful career, he and Deena thought perhaps the inklings were a hint that he should go into politics. "That seemed like the avenue that God was calling him for," Deena recalled. "But something about that didn't feel right, so he continued praying and we continued with our conversations about what he thought God's plan was.

"About a year before he was killed, Tom came to me and said, 'I don't know what's going to happen, but I have a feeling that you have always thought I was going to die young.' I was surprised because I never talked to him about it. I asked him why he thought that and he said, 'I don't know, but it may have something to do with God's plan for me. I'm not sure why I think that. But I need you to tell me what you think.' I said, 'Well, I just always believed that we were not going to grow old together, that something was going to happen to prevent us from growing old together. One of us is going to be killed.'

"*He took me seriously,*" recalled Deena. "It was a serious conversation. We knew that we had to be prepared. He went out the next day and tried to double the life insurance on both of us. This was the September before. He was able to double mine but not his because he had been diagnosed with sleep apnea earlier that year. To make a long story short, we just proceeded dreaming our dreams and living our lives and working toward our goals, but having an over-riding fear that something was going to happen to one of us.

"My feeling was that it was going to be Tom, and Tom's feeling was that it was going to be him. He just felt that whatever God's plan was for him, it had something to do with the White House and was going to impact a lot of people."

Then came September 11. Burnett was on a business trip to New York City and on his return he found himself in the first-class section of a plane at Newark Airport — surrounded, it turned out, by terrorists. About 45 minutes into the flight, he called Deena on his cell phone. When she asked if he was okay, Tom said, "No, I'm not. I'm on an airplane that has been hijacked."

Just a couple minutes before four terrorists had burst into the cockpit and apparently killed the crew. They also had knifed a passenger and herded the rest to the back of the plane — where Burnett and others formulated their famous plan to overtake the hijackers before the plane could reach its presumed target: Washington, and possibly the White House!

Her heart pounding, Deena contacted the FBI to let them know what was happening. When Tom next called, he reported that the wounded passenger was dead. Deena told him about the other hijacked planes and how two had hit the World Trade Center. "Oh my God, it's a suicide mission," she heard him tell his seatmate as she filled him in on what little else was known.

It was at this point that Tom noticed the plane turning back east. At first he thought it was headed for New York. But then he realized it was going southeast. "We're over a rural area," he told his wife. "It's fields. I've *gotta go.*"

He was a take-charge kind of guy, a 6' 2" former football star in high school back in Bloomington, Minnesota, and Deena immediately knew that he was going to try to stop the hijackers.

Such was confirmed the next time he called from his cell phone.

"They're talking about crashing this plane into the ground," Tom told her. "We have to do something. I'm putting a plan together." The last time he phoned he said, "We're going to take back the plane. We can't wait for the authorities. I don't know what they could do anyway. It's up to us. I think we can do it."

"What do you want me to do?" Deena, a believing Baptist, had asked.

"Pray, Denna," said Tom. *"Just pray."*

And that they did.

"The two of us were calm — eerily calm," she recalled. "I knew that no matter what happened, everything was going to be okay. I remember after hanging up the phone following each conversation with him just saying the same prayer. I asked God to hold him in the palms of His Hands. I prayed for strength for all of us and the endurance to do God's Will."

Deena said that when she and other relatives listened to the flight's "black box" afterwards, she could hear her husband barking directives as they indeed tried to overcome the hijackers.

"I know that he motivated those people aboard that flight to do what they did," says Deena. "And I also know that had he not been on the plane, that circumstances would have been very different today."

Chapter 17

God hears every thought and sees every tear

No one knows exactly where Flight 93 would have struck. It could have been the U.S. Capitol, the White House, or the C.I.A. The point is that *something prophetic had been uttered* to Burnett and he had acted on it (as had the other heroes aboard that plane, perhaps altering the course of history).

God prepares us all, if usually in a far less dramatic way. We are not all called to martyrdom.

But when we act on intuition, it affects our lives.

Intuition is interaction with Him, when it has been confirmed through prayer.

God doesn't usually reveal much of what He has in mind for us (somehow this would spoil the "test"), but He does grant necessary *indications*. Look at Deena: she just "felt" something about their not growing old together. I mentioned infusions of thought. This is the most common way that the Holy Spirit gives us inspiration. In the spirit world are angels whose job it is to warn and prompt us, to inspire us, and many events in history have been affected by it. Such has been acknowledged by scientists like Thomas Edison – who had such a sense of a transcendental force that he spent his last years trying to invent a device to more directly communicate with spirits (something that of course is not advisable).

Few are those who know that Isaac Newton was so spiritually involved that he kept notes for fifty years on his view of the Apocalypse.

Apparently he too sensed that his ideas came from elsewhere.

But mainly it is the common folk to whom Heaven speaks to prepare us or to console. We receive signs from the other side. A remarkable story comes from Virginia Giovanello of Brockton, Massachusetts, who was devastated by the death of an aunt named Lola.

"My Aunt Lola lived downstairs and was very special to me — I resemble her and sometimes people thought she was my mother," Virginia told me. "She was my godmother and like a second mother to me. Aunt Lola died five minutes after midnight, on Christmas day, in 1997, after the Pope's Mass, with the choir singing *Silent Night* on every TV throughout the rehab hospital.

"Every Christmas, I dress up like Mrs. Claus at my school on the last day before Christmas vacation. Needless to say, come 1998, I didn't feel like dressing up for the kids because Christmas was not a happy season for me. But the night before the last day of school, I had a dream, and I saw Auntie Lola sitting in the living room, with her sister, Lena, standing in the background. Lola had a Christmas green sweater *with a red something on it*. She was waving happily to me with lots of energy. When I woke up that morning, I was still not going to dress up as Mrs. Claus. When I got out of the shower, I reluctantly thought about dressing up, not wanting to disappoint the students, but I couldn't anyway because I didn't have a red bow to wear on the collar. Somehow it was missing from the outfit.

"For some reason, I went downstairs to Aunt Lola's bedroom and sat on the bed and sobbed my heart out, just wanting to be with her. Seeing her in the dream was wonderful, but I wasn't as happy about it as *she* appeared to be.

"Then I got up from the bed and turned around because I saw something red in the mirror. Behind me, on the bed, was the perfect red bow. I was filled with a feeling I can't describe! Whenever I needed an outfit, Auntie Lola always had an accessory or the right blouse, and she still was primping me!

"I donned my outfit, and had more Christmas spirit than I ever had! I thought I would get into trouble at school, because the students tend to wander about the school on that day, filled with excitement, and I had so many kids in my room, it was bursting, and the love that was permeating the air was overwhelming! After school, I spread that love and cheer all over town! I will never forget that day... and I am assured that God hears every thought and sees every tear. He certainly sent the troops out that day to get me out of doldrums and I fell right into His loving Hands! I guess somebody knew that I wasn't going to be Mrs. Claus that year and made sure that it was going to happen!"

Chapter 18

Signs and confirmations

Although we are never to initiate contact with the deceased (see *Deuteronomy* 18:11), I have little doubt that on occasion those on the other side are allowed to send us signals. Usually we interact with the supernatural without knowing it.

But there are the striking cases. There is the woman whose son had been known as "Red." He died at a young age of epilepsy. Time after time, following his death, red cardinals would sweep near his mother. Once when she was feeling especially down (wailing near a tree dedicated to his memory), a beautiful red one flew within five feet of her. In England a woman who was likewise depressed suddenly saw the sun erupt through the rain, causing rainbow-like reflections on a tree. "I never saw anything like that before," she recalled. "I called my daughter to have a look at that beautiful sight. We watched about an hour. It was a very beautiful experience. It looked like 'singing colors.' It lifted my heart right up to God. I thanked Him for giving me a lovely surprise."

"I was going through a very difficult time in my life," related another woman, Diane Duffin of Sciutate, Massachusetts. "A single mom with three teenage sons, I had just taken a high-pressure job and moved my family — including my mother — to a new state. Daily I saw abuses of corporate power that greatly disturbed me. At the same time, my work pressures mounted, and I worried about my family feeling lonely and disconnected. Coming home after a very taxing day, I decided to walk on the beach to clear my head. As I charged along the deserted beach, my mind was racing and I was asking God a thousand questions. Finally, I asked for some kind of answer, even just one word, anything that would help me make sense of everything. I heard nothing. Again I asked. Silence. Impatient, I put the question another way: 'Jesus, if you were walking down this beach, and we met, and I told you everything going on in my life, what would you say to me?' Silence. I turned sadly to walk back home, then suddenly I looked down at the sand and in large deeply etched letters right in front of my feet was written: *'I love you!'* with the exclamation point. I looked up at the sky and started to cry. I realized it was all I needed to know."

When Joyce Hayden of Glassboro, New Jersey, felt stressed, she prayed for someone to help her and spotted a mailbox with the name "Godshall"!

Another time, financially pressed — praying to make it to the next pay day, and wondering about her future — she stared out the window as a semi-truck drove past with the words "G.O.D. Delivers."

Signs come in many ways, and the more we pray, the more regular they become.

I know a woman who was fretting over her husband's loss of a job when a button dropped from her cardigan and rolled across the garden, landing next to what she thought was a little stone.

It turned out to be another button (looking very weather-beaten) from the very same cardigan, which she had lost three years before! She took it as a sign that God was near her.

The same was true of a woman from Momence, Illinois, named Mary Zink, who said, "My sister was murdered in 1986. While saying the Rosary in front of a picture of the Immaculate and Sorrowful Heart of Mary, as I was crying and missing my sister, I said, 'Lord in my spiritual strength I know my sister is in Heaven, but in my human weakness I am asking you for a sign.' As I said those words I felt a peaceful presence and heard an audible voice. 'I am an angel of God. The Lord wishes to grant your request for a sign that your sister is in Heaven. You will become pregnant and your child will be born on your sister's birthday. This is the sign not only that your sister is in Heaven but a sign of the love that the Lord has for you and for her.' My youngest child was born on her birthday in 1990."

Others have found comfort in music. Some call it coincidence. Some call it synchronicity. What it really is, of course, is the coordination of God.

"There is a song that plays a big part in my family's life," said Mary Jane Haley of Maryland. "It was chosen by my son to be the song he and his wife danced to at their wedding. I can't remember the name of the song by Garth Brooks, but one line goes, 'I could have missed the pain but I would have had to miss the dance.' We thought it an odd song for a wedding but he loved that song. This beloved son passed away ten years later, in 2000, at 36 years of age," Mary Jane continued. "Now whenever his wife is troubled or needs reassurance, she will suddenly hear that song on the car radio, on a TV show — wherever she might be. She knows then that Joe is watching over her and their two children."

As with other miracles, communication with God is like rolling a snowball down a hill. It grows larger as we build faith. I didn't think there could be a better phone story than the one involving that payphone in Ohio, but in fact there is a case that is equally spectacular, demonstrating the power of persistence right to the end.

It involves a Tennesse man named Vincent Tan, who suddenly woke one night in 1996 at 4:30 a.m. with a burden to pray. He did so, fell back asleep, and then arose at seven a.m. to pray again. Shortly after, the phone rang, and for some reason, his answering machine didn't pick up. And the phone kept ringing. Vincent decided to answer himself, even though the call identification was also not functioning. "Hello," he said, and surprisingly, the other party also said "Hello," as if likewise answering. When Vincent asked the woman if she wanted to speak to him, she said no. She was just answering her phone! When he asked why she called, she said she didn't – her phone had simply rung, and she had answered it. It turned out that her name was Doris and she was in Iowa. Somehow, their lines had crossed. Astonishingly, when she heard Vincent's full name, she recognized him as a man she had read about as having had an experience years before with an angel. She went on to say that six months previously her mother had been diagnosed with cancer, had been given only six months to live, and had prayed to one day meet this man who had the angel experience! Doris explained to Tan that in her prayers the ill woman had cited the passage from *Jeremiah* 32:27: "Behold, I am the Lord, the God of all flesh: is there anything too hard for me?" She went on to tell Tan that her mother was very near death and that at 3:30 a.m. Iowa time – 4:30 a.m. Vincent's time – she had awakened and felt called to remind the Lord of her mother's request – to speak with Tan!

She asked if Vincent would speak to her mom, Vincent agreed, they set up the speaker phone (the woman was bed-ridden) and after Tan spoke to her, repeating his angel account in its entirety, the woman said, "praise the Lord. Amen."

That was followed by a long strange silence, and when Doris got back on the phone, it was to say that her mother had just passed away!

Hope beyond hope. Persistence beyond persistence.

Faith can do anything and lead anywhere. Where faith begins, fear ends. As with every other attribute, the way to increase it is to practice it constantly. It is never wasted. We toss it like seed and some of it takes great root. As Scripture tells us, developing faith is like planting the seeds of the mustard tree. Those are among the tiniest seeds, but when nurtured they grow into an awesome plant, the bark impenetrable, the branches reaching heavenward, the roots able to split rocks. If you want to crack open a mountain – if you want to move a rock — listen to what God has to say.

Any time we have faith we get blessed and anytime we plant there will be a harvest, somehow, in some way. The better we become at it, the larger the harvest will grow. Even if some things don't pan out — even if certain prayers aren't "answered" — we still receive benefits. The Lord may not answer precisely the way we designed, nor right away, but if so, it's because it is not what is best for us at that particular moment. Still, it goes into a spiritual "bank account."

God keeps track of our faithfulness and adds "interest" each time we exercise it. Satan tries to rub our noses in the negative. We have to always reject his "evil reports." Don't listen to him. Don't listen to the store clerk who makes a comment that causes an unintentional sting, that mentions something that bothers you, that brings something to mind that you are trying to forget.

When we practice faith in both large and small things, when we are constant, and when we never allow discouragement, we can expect a harvest or series of harvests. Sometimes, it comes gradually; sometimes, it takes a while. But it comes because it's inevitable. *No exercise of faith is wasted.* If we maintain trust in all things — if we keep exercising it, if we keep tossing those seeds, relentlessly — it's only a matter of time before a big prayer is answered by signs.

We must exercise caution, of course: as it says in Scripture, a generation that tests God by asking for a sign – that is, requesting one for the wrong reason, such as trying to make God prove Himself – is a corrupt generation. At the same time, it is an adulterous generation that ignores the legitimate signs from Heaven. "God speaks quietly," Pope Benedict XVI once wrote. "But He gives us all kinds of signs. In retrospect, especially, we can see that He has given us a little nudge through a friend, through a book, or through what we see as a failure – even through 'accidents.' Life is actually full of these silent indications. If we remain alert, then slowly they piece together a consistent whole, and we begin to feel how God is guiding us."

It seems to be the case that we can ask for signs *as long as we are not testing God.* Some call it "confirmations." There are examples in Scripture. But in due course, God sends them anyway, and to everyone. Even those who profess no religion are often swayed by what might be called "meaningful coincidences." God has an old friend call just as you're thinking of that old buddy or places someone in your path who says what you needed to know at that moment. Or He leads you to an article or scripture with an especially pertinent verse.

These are signs, but we are not to treat them as augurs – as a method of fortunetelling — and we should never become obsessed with them. The authentic ones occur spontaneously; we cannot call up such signs at will. In the Old Testament, most of the omens were large events like those brought against the pharaoh or attendant to Moses while in the New Testament the "signs" usually refer to the charisms of the disciples: healing, casting out demons, speaking in tongues.

When we pursue these, we are in the flow of the Holy Spirit, and when we are in the flow of the Holy Spirit, God sends His indications much more readily.

The greatest signs are always how we feel *internally*.

They are markers sent from Heaven, and they often manifest in the way that things go – as I said, whether they are easy or not so easy. Although resistance sometimes comes from the enemy, or simply from the tests of life, when there are too *many* roadblocks in striving for what you want — when you are banging your head against a wall too often, when nothing is falling into place, or when you are unsure and can't gain certainty, despite prayer — what you're doing is probably not in God's plan. Look toward your stomach and you will feel whether something sits well. The Lord's Spirit works through all our members in subtle communication.

There may be other kinds of indications. Before we moved, we lived in a home with the office in the basement. It was a nice workplace, but it was still a basement, and so it was dark. For years we had been contemplating a move, possibly to Florida, where many ministries are located. We felt "called." But naturally we were tossing it around. One day coming up from the basement after a long day's work we turned on the television and began to watch a re-run of Archbishop Fulton Sheen, the famous evangelist in the Sixties. Ironically, we had just placed a video of him for sale on our website. It was peculiar because we don't usually watch television.

But there we were, watching it, both of us glued to the talented bishop, when suddenly, out of the blue, he said something like, "Come out of that basement!" I'm not even sure what he was alluding to. We were startled – and all the more so when, a few minutes later, speaking of the cold northeastern winters (he was based in Upstate New York), he said something like, "take a trip to California – or go to Florida." We felt he was speaking to us right through that television set!

When we did move to Florida, virtually every major event occurred on a feast day. We got the offer for our home on the Feast of the Assumption, the first day we had the for-sale sign up. We received the purchase agreement days later, on the feast of Our Lady of Knock, where I had been on pilgrimage. As I recall, we signed the agreement the next day — on the Queenship of Mary. I went down to Florida to secure a lot on the feast of Our Lady of LaSalette, where I also had been, and we were sent our purchase agreement for the construction of our new home on September 29 — which is the feast of my patron, the Archangel Michael.

Every day is a day for certain saints, but these all were major feasts that went beyond coincidence. Throughout the move we asked for the intercession of St. Joseph, and as it turned out my in-laws, who moved with us, closed on their house the week of St. Joseph's feast – in fact, the check probably cleared on his very day! By "coincidence," a statue of him happened to be on the dining room table (set there out of reach of our baby) where they signed the final papers.

We didn't plan that but the way things had gone, we were confused that the actual day of our own closing was not going to be a major feast day — only to realize later that it was the Feast of St. Lucy and it was a woman named Lucy who was buying our home! When we finally moved, we were hoping it would be May 13, which is an anniversary attached to the apparition at Fatima. The movers couldn't swing that, but later they had a change in schedule and ended up leaving our old house on May 13!

Chapter 19

In His Name you can heal

Not that we engineered the move based on signs. That would be dangerous. The devil is only too happy to come in and manipulate.

But at times God lends us guidance through signs, and we are to inte-
grate these signs into our general inclinations.

Remember, God sees where all the pieces to the puzzle go, while we
get hung up on a single piece. Or we try to make an entirely new puzzle,
one that is more to our own liking. When we do that, however, the pieces
don't fit. When we lack faith, we find ourselves forcing issues, which causes
breakage.

This is a sure sign that we have strayed from where God wants us and
if we keep it up, something will give. It may work for a while (we may be
able to "push things through"), but when we strain, there are defects around
what we do. It will not bear the kind of fruit that comes when we're walking with the Spirit.

When you run across a pushy person, how do *you* feel? Don't you
want to be contrary, just for the sake of being contrary? Don't you resist
that person? Now imagine how God feels. We're meant to work within the
framework of what He has designed for us, and when we don't, there is
resistance because we are pushing ourselves beyond his blueprints.

Think of what happens when scientists try to alter or stretch His creation.
We end up with toxic chemical waste that is carcinogenic.

Similar trash piles up in us as long as we're out of God's Will and
ignoring His attempts at communication. The Lord grants us plenty of direction, and the same is true of animals. In their case we call it "instinct."
From birth, many animals have all the knowledge they need to survive: God
gives animals capabilities that seem almost supernormal. They know how
to fly or search out food and are incredible at avoiding enemies. There are
animals that look like a twig or leaf or that can hide by changing color. They
have been granted terrific camouflage. And they possess such phenomenal
capabilities right from birth. Did you ever try to catch a minnow with your
bare hands? A baby fish instantly knows to swim away from a human. A
spider knows how to spin a web. A bee knows to head for pollen. Ants know

how to build a "castle" without anyone designing it for them.

These are gifts from God, and we know we're hearing from God when we have knowledge that is innate. Isn't it a miracle that tortoises know how to dig tunnels and squirrels how to store food at just the right time of year, bears how to hibernate? Isn't it remarkable that birds fly south? Even when something unusual is approaching, animals sense it and know exactly how to prepare. No matter how intense a storm, it's rare to see it kill large numbers of birds or any other wild animals, who know where and how to shield themselves even if they have never faced such a storm before, as if they have a sixth sense. A dog will often howl when its owner dies, and when the tsunami hit Asia in 2004, scientists were amazed at how few animals died; virtually all escaped.

God instills knowledge in ways we don't understand and also gives humans the urge to do or not to do certain things in life, as a matter of survival. How interesting it is how the things that disgust, repel, or cause automatic fear (spiders!) often have a dangerous element. We have an eerie feeling around rough water – which could cause us to drown. We feel "creepy" around snakes – which can be venomous. We can't stand insects or rodents, which can transmit *Yersinia pestis* (the bacteria behind bubonic fever) or West Nile virus. We're revolted by excretions, which can carry harmful bacteria.

There are reasons we feel the way we do (it's in the design, the warning system, of God), and He miraculously transmits these instincts. There is an Intelligence to our very cells. "It's" called God. If that doesn't work, He gives us a stronger prompting. We could also call this a "knowing": We all have had the experience of *knowing* something isn't good, or *knowing* we shouldn't go somewhere, or *knowing* we should look to the left (only to see a car coming). Many are those who have avoided catastrophe when their plans were changed at the last moment.

As we struggle to get through this adventure called life we have to take advantage of Godly communication. Sometimes that communication is very direct. We recall Moses. In our own time are many folks like Bob Rice of Santa Fe, New Mexico, a former pastor who first began a healing ministry as a 26-year-old truck driver living in Vista, California, due to a startling locution. Raised a Baptist, Rice was a lukewarm believer and former Marine when one night he "heard" a voice speak to him in his thoughts. He took it to be God, Who gave him the name of a specific place he had never heard of. "The voice woke me up, and told me He wanted me to go to the 'Full

Gospel Rescue Mission' in San Diego," claims Rice.

Unsure what to make of it — and not one for mystical knowledge — this young man tried to push it out of his mind until the "voice" spoke a second time on the same day. When that happened, Rice decided to do as he was told and headed with a friend to San Diego, where they looked in the part of town they thought might have a rescue mission.

It was the beginning of what turns out to be an astonishing journey, for they not only found a rescue mission but one by the exact name Bob had been "given"!

When they entered, Rice explained what had happened to a cook at the mission. Later he did the same with the pastor — who shocked Rice by asking him to speak during the service that night.

Of course, he had never done anything of the like. He had no idea how to preach. But the young truck driver did as he was told and took to the pulpit. "I didn't know what I was going to do," he recalls. "When I got to the pulpit I opened my Bible and just laid it down — opened to no particular place, because I didn't know anything about it. I prayed a very simple prayer — telling the Lord that these were His people and that if there was any way He could use me, there I was. Use me."

In those simple, heartfelt words, Rice had surrendered and had done so with blind faith.

"Then I had this one thought going through my mind. I didn't know if it was Scripture or something I had read, but there was this thought going through my mind, and when I looked back down at my Bible, I couldn't believe my eyes: I began to read the same words that were in my thoughts. It was *Mark* 16:17 — where it says signs shall follow those who believe, that 'in My Name they shall cast out devils, they shall speak with new tongues... they shall lay hands upon the sick and they shall recover.'"

Then the "voice" returned. This time he heard the words, "Bob, there's a woman out there tonight who's blind and I want to restore her sight."

When Rice asked the crowd if there was any such person, a woman in the back corner raised her hand, indicating that she was the one who was blind.

"Scared stiff," Rice did what came instinctively — directing the woman to come forward and asking if she believed that she could be healed.

When she said yes, Rice reached out (again, by instinct), touched the woman's forehead, and in a commanding tone said, "In the Name of Jesus, receive your sight!" This was a guy who wasn't even a strong Sunday churchgoer!

But Bob was operating on faith (which had dispelled his fear), and the next thing he knew, the lady was lying on the floor. "I said, 'Oh, my God, what have I done now!' I had never seen anyone rest in the Spirit. It was the first time. A few seconds later, she started to cry out, *'I can see! I can see!'*

A blind woman had regained her sight instantly.

"Then the same voice spoke to me again and said there was a man who was deaf in his left ear. I saw what happened the first time and decided to try it again."

Announcing that he had just been "told" there was a man with the ear problem, Rice now watched as another hand flew into the air and a man stepped forward, announcing that he was the one. Rice asked in astonishment if he believed he could be healed, the man said yes, and so Bob repeated the prayer — touching the man on the forehead.

"Boom," Rice recalls. "He was lying on the floor. Here this guy is lying on the floor and he got up a few minutes later and he had his hearing!"

Chapter 20

Often, it is evil that causes illness

We do have to discern: It's dangerous to start sitting around believing that God or any spirit is telling us every single thing we should do. As I said, God normally communicates softly, without actual words. To seek after fantastic communication is to open oneself to deception.

But to forget that we can communicate with God is even more tragic. We exist, after all, by every Word He has spoken; it was His Word (see *Genesis*) that formed our existence.

He speaks in countless ways.

There were two privates in World War II. They were stationed in France. One asked the other to watch his rosary. He gave it to the second soldier because he figured he was more likely to survive, which turned out to be true. They never saw each other again, but the private kept his promise to get the rosary back to his family and searched for them for decades. When he himself died at a ripe old age, his widow continued the search and after what was a combined sixty-year hunt, she discovered that relatives of the first soldier – the one who died in combat – lived next door to her!

Only God does things like that. The message?

Faith over a long period ends with the spectacular.

While not seeking the fantastic, we must listen during prayer. Here we receive our intuition, and the clarity increases in proportion to *how clear our spirits are*. As John Paul II said, "the illuminative stage of the interior life emerges gradually from the purgative stage." That is worth reading a second time.

Think of it like a stream. When there is debris, it slows the influx of water and causes stagnation. Think of logs. Sins accumulate, and when they collect to a certain point, there is a logjam. Jesus told us to remove those logs and when we don't, they block the Spirit.

With each transgression there is an additional blot in our souls and each blot opens the way for evil (whether actual harassment by the dark side or the infliction of ailments).

There is such a thing as redemptive suffering, but most manifestations come from the force of darkness. In *James* 5:14 it instructs us to "confess your sins to one another and pray for one another, so that you will be healed."

The God of Miracles

In *Psalms* (107:17) we are told, "Some were fools, suffering because of their sins and because of their evil." In *Jeremiah* 5:25 we hear that "your sins have kept these good things from you." As it says in *Ephesians* (4:26-27), "Be ye angry and sin not; let not the sun go down upon your wrath: neither give place to the devil."

Sin gives the devil a legal right and blocks God's blessings!

In so doing we invite in the evil spirit, who, as Christ showed, is the destroyer — a murder from the beginning, the spirit of affliction.

Name him. Cast him out by description. Throw the devil out in the Name of Jesus!

There are spirits of failure and spirits of distress and spirits of loneliness and phobias and just about anything negative. If you are in a snare and going around and around, if you are on a treadmill — if you can't break out of a negative cycle — cast away the personal force that may be binding you. Often this is crucial before there can be a healing.

Do so during Mass. Do so while praying the Stations of the Cross. Do so especially while receiving the Precious Blood. If it is a severe case, do so under the guidance of a priest.

We all die, yes, but God wants you whole and to have the fullness of years. He doesn't want you wasting away. When that happens, especially in youth, the focus must be on casting out the spirit of sickness or whatever spirit may be afflicting you. As Scripture indicates, such spirits come in countless ways — through family lines, through our own darkness, through the course of worldly interactions. The prince of this world is Satan and Jesus came to defeat his works (among them infirmity). That's why we see in *Isaiah* 53: 4-5 — in the prophecy of His Coming — that it says "through His stripes we are healed."

Christ died for our sins and that implies that He also died for our infirmities. He is the Great Healer. Says *Matthew* 8:17, "He did this to make come true what the prophet Isaiah had said, 'He Himself took our sickness and carried away our diseases.'"

Such is all but ignored in our times, when the secular has pervaded Christianity and quashed the Spirit. Many Church leaders dismiss the idea of supernatural healing! Yet it is time to reflect upon Scripture. "Bless the Lord, O my soul," says *Psalms* 103:2-3, "and forget not all his benefits: Who forgiveth all thine iniquities; Who healeth all thy diseases."

To get unblocked it is crucial to address the issue head on and not to fear. "We know that fear is not from the Lord. For God hath not given us the spirit of fear..." notes 2 *Timothy* 1:7.

"For the thing which I greatly feared is come upon me, and that which I was afraid of is come unto me," says *Job* 3:25.

Fear attracts the negative. It attracts what you are fearing!

When we get rid of fear — which may be the block — a whole new world opens before us (a world of brightness, a world of healing).

For some, purgatory is suffered here on earth. There are martyrs. Again, there is redemptive suffering. There was Job himself. Paul suffered a thorn in his side. Jesus demonstrated that there is suffering on this earth when He told us to carry our own crosses on a daily basis. When He suffered, it was according to the Will (or "cup") of the Father.

But too often it's a simple block, not God's Will, and we need to get *un*blocked, believing in the power of God no matter what religious "experts" say.

For what occurs in the soul is reflected in the physical.

One who is rigid and unbending may find that manifest as stiff arthritic joints and one who is hard of heart may develop coronary problems, and someone who is hardheaded may fall victim to migraines.

Does that imply that everyone with atherosclerosis is hard of heart? Or that everyone with a headache is stubborn? No. But it means that what occurs in the spiritual prefigures the physical. Evil can find a weakness, exacerbating an existing condition. There are ministers who assert that a spiritual burden can lead to a hunched back.

Often we use expressions that are more accurate than we know. Something "makes us sick." There is "bad bile." We are "worried to death." Be careful what you say. More than anything, be careful what you *believe*.

I know of atheists who had to "die" before they developed faith, and I mean this literally. In one case, a doctor in Moscow was hit by the car and in such a comatose state that he was whisked to the morgue before he revived. His name was George Rodonaia, and when he succumbed he was shocked to find that although he "died," he had maintained consciousness and found himself in a place of blackness. He ended up becoming a minister in Texas.

Chapter 21

Step back from your 'test'

God is perfect and He knows perfectly well what's best for you and will redound to your eternity. We won't see the whole picture until we are on the "other side."

Some miracles are impossible to deny.

There is the example of a doctor named Ann Kay Logarbo in Louisiana whose grand-niece, six-year-old Caroline, had spent two days in the hospital suffering horrible seizures caused by encephalitis. From her training Dr. Logarbo knew that the girl was probably brain-damaged — unable to breathe for herself — and soon would die a horrible death.

But Dr. Logarbo let go – knew there was nothing more that could be medically done – and discovered that God was more effective. Deeply religious, her family prayed for the intercession of a local priest, Father Francis Xavier Seelos, whose cause had been put forward for canonization.

That was a Monday afternoon.

Months later, when Dr. Logarbo looked back at Caroline's medical records, she could see what other doctors couldn't – that Caroline's vital signs began to improve in the same hour. Dr. Logarbo had receded to a corner and told God that she could not do any more, that she could not go on like this. There was no one who could save her niece. The only way she was going to survive, the only way the girl was going to be given back to them, acknowledged Dr. Logarbo, was "God's intervention."

Suddenly the doctor felt an excruciating pain in her chest, and while it quickly went away, it was like a wake-up.

She felt a "pull" to check the intensive-care unit.

When she did, she found that the little girl was now miraculously aware, could respond to the command to blink — and by 9 a.m. was able to open her eyes and follow a Crucifix. An exam by startled doctors showed that the girl could also respond to commands to move her legs and arms. By 5 p.m., neurologists had decided that the girl would live, but would never walk or talk again. They also decided that she would require a year in the hospital.

But on the Catholic Feast of the Assumption — which was eight days later — Caroline was discharged, walking *and* talking.

"Medically, there was no explanation for the recovery of Caroline," said this doctor who stepped back and leaned on God.

Hope is present at all levels of faith – before and during and after we have developed truly deep trust – and surrender takes it all a giant step in the miraculous direction. Surrender and trust are the *crucial* high levels of faith. Note how it plays into so many miracles I am recounting.

To do that we often have to rid emotions that come from the self (where so much fear resides) and step back.

To step back is not to avoid a test, but to rise above it. It is to surrender.

We have to separate ourselves from the negative.

To separate is to place a distance.

Allow God to fill the vacuum!

Let's say you get a zinging e-mail from someone. There is the opportunity for irritation, even anger. Someone has insulted you. It can be really cutting, and usually it catches us off guard, if we immediately allow ourselves to be engaged by it. That's why we need prayer for the presence of mind – so we react in a way that is collected, instead of instinctive. The first response to a negative situation will often be the determining factor. Irritation can quickly root. If we let it, the sting will remain. Instead, the first reaction to a challenging circumstance has to be to step back from the issue, strive to understand the frailties of whoever sent it (if it is an insult), and forgive that person immediately.

Recognize it as a "good test" of your new spiritual mettle. And every time an irritating thought enters your mind, get in the habit of realizing it for what it is and thanking God for it.

Your faith will grow and you'll experience less stress.

You'll also come to realize that stress is worry and worry is the opposite of faith. When we're stressed, it's because we have fallen back into the old lie that *we're* in charge and therefore *we* must work out every single detail (and fret over each one for good measure).

Chapter 22

'Unlove' is the road to darkness

To step back is to realize that there is no perfection in this world and that trying to make everything perfect is the root of stress. Rely on God. *Don't strain unless it is absolutely necessary.* When we strain, it's like adding too much heat when we bake. Instead of something sweet we have something that is black and bitter.

There are situations in which we *must* place ourselves under a certain amount of pressure (times when we have to be urgent), but even then, in the midst of a crisis, in the "frenzy," the best thing to do is take a deep breath, utter a prayer (slowly), and *step back.* Our first response should always be to step back and utter the name "Jesus" (prayerfully).

That automatically backs us up, prevents a premature engagement with forces of darkness (which *want* us in a frenzy), and allows us to more clearly assess a circumstance.

To avoid frenzy, we must also be very wary of the media. There is much negativity on television, in songs, in movies, on the radio, and on the internet. The very intrusion of such energy into your home can upset the spiritual dynamic.

Our society is at a breakpoint because we are fed dark electronic negativity constantly. This also comes by way of talk shows in which commentators point out the failings of others.

Anything obsessive or negative is counter-miraculous (especially when the obsession is about the fault of another).

When someone is overly critical, this is a sign of pride, which, as I can't emphasize enough, is a dangerous imperfection. How many arrogant and critical people have you known, and what eventually happened to them? Did they not ride high for a while, until circumstances arrived that caused humiliation?

What we say and even think about others comes back to haunt us. Whatever you do, don't let a setback draw you into a mode of the negative. I have emphasized that we must not besmirch others. It is important not to criticize.

It's a spiritual axiom — what goes around comes around — and *love(not criticality) is the vocation of humans.* We are given different ways of accomplishing that mission. Each time we assist another, instead of criticizing, each time we pray for an enemy, is a big deal to Jesus.

To despise and hate is to descend into darkness. Nothing is more likely to distance us from God, and that distance can be fatal. We have the account of a man I know named Dr. Howard Storm, who was head of the art department at North Kentucky University. Professor Storm was once such an ardent atheist that he ridiculed a Baptist secretary in his office. A rude, arrogant man (by his own description), he was cruel to her and barely tolerated a nun who took his course, warning her to keep all mention of God out of his classroom.

A "diehard" atheist, he "died hard" all right — of a ruptured duodenum – and found himself in a foggy place that led, he now believes, to the "cesspool of the universe."

That's one of the most painful things that can happen to you – a ruptured intestine, which causes the acid to seep into your other organs — and it occurred on June 1, 1985, as Professor Storm was leading an art excursion in Paris. Rushed to a hospital, he suffered agonizing pain for nine hours (while waiting for a surgeon), and when the surgeon didn't come, when they couldn't find one who was available, when he knew his body couldn't hold up for another minute, Dr. Storm turned to his wife, a prominent attorney, kissed her good-bye, and turned over to meet his death, sure that there would be nothing but blackness. "As certain as you can be certain of anything" that it would be "lights out," Storm rolled on his side and prepared to enter nothingness.

But a moment later, to Storm's shock, he suddenly found himself out of his body – standing at the foot of the bed — *staring at his corpse.*

Why was his wife crying? He tried to speak with her. She couldn't hear him. He tried to speak to the patient next to him. No go there either. He saw his own body on the bed and stared at the corpse, wondering how it could be *there* while he – or at least his consciousness — was at the foot of the bed. Had they created a mold of his body for some reason?

Everything around him looked strange. The colors were different and he was in the hospital but not *really* in the hospital. The hall was now more like a misty passage – filled with fog, as was the case with Rodaia – and he was being summoned there. He heard voices urging him to come along and saying that they had been waiting for him.

Despite initial trepidation, Dr. Storm did just that, heading for the voices and following them down the haze-filled "hall," which seemed to slowly slope downward. He couldn't see anyone, and the farther they went, the more demanding the voices became. Soon, they became outright aggressive, and then hostile. When they showed themselves out of the mist, Storm was horrified to see that he was in the company of what looked like former humans with some bestial characteristics, including longer bicuspid teeth and pointy fingernails. These beings began to ridicule him, then humiliate him, and finally to attack Storm, ripping at his "flesh" in a horrendous fashion.

It was terrifying, and he also knew it was "going to get a lot worse." He realized he was in a sewer headed for "the cosmic cesspool." A little voice told him to pray, but that was crazy, he thought; he was an atheist. But Storm was also in terror, and scrambling, he tried to think of a prayer. None came to mind. He tried to think of anything with "God" in it. Desperate, he cited the Pledge of Allegiance — noticing that the mention of God caused the creatures to back away. Then he recalled a ditty from Sunday school: "Jesus loves me this I know."

And he was amazed when that caused the creatures to dash back into the fog!

Jesus, *Jesus*.

He kept repeating it, and soon Dr. Storm saw what he thought was a comet. Now there was a new fear: he thought he was going to be hit. It was coming right for him. There was no doubt that it was directed his way. A light. A blazing, streaking light. But instead of hitting him, the luminosity stopped in front of Storm and drew him out of the "cesspool."

Suddenly, Howard was in what seemed like outer space, and the Light was Jesus, speaking to him. So powerful was the experience that afterward, Storm too would become a minister. Soon he was placed in the company of three angels, who reviewed his life. To Dr. Storm, this was nearly as painful as anything else. Although the angels didn't do so in a condemning manner, they showed him all the times he had been mean to people and he was made to feel the way he had made others feel. This is quite common in such experiences: that the person who "dies" is evaluated on how he made others feel, and experiences both the joy and sorrow caused to others. We experience both the dignity we gave others or the lack thereof. No doubt, Storm was given to feel the way that secretary and the nun had felt. "People who were religious were kidding themselves," had been Storm's perspective. "I viewed them with contempt. I thought they believed in fairy tales because they couldn't cope with the harsh reality of life. They bought into fantasy to justify their mediocrity. If that's what it takes to make them feel good, let them wallow in it. I was in the mainstream of my culture. I had no faith, no hope, and no reliance on anyone, just survival of the fittest. My colleagues at the university (the ones I associated with) thought the way I did about life. I was in good company. Man was the measure of all things. I was in control of my life."

That was until he encountered the angels, who showed Dr. Storm what his life really had been about.

"The record of my life was their record, not my memory of life," he later wrote of the angels. "We watched and experienced episodes that were from the point of view of a third party. The scenes they showed me were often incidents I had forgotten. They showed effects on people's lives of which I had no previous knowledge. They reported thoughts and feelings of people I had interacted with which I had been unaware of at the time. They showed me scenes from my life that I would not have chosen and they eliminated scenes from my life that I wanted them to see. It was a complete surprise how my life history was presented before us. I believed that my worth was measured by my success in my chosen career. When the angels showed me how destructive this careerism was to the well-being of my loved ones, I wanted to end my life review. They insisted that I needed to see the truth of my life and learn from it. I begged them to stop it because I was so ashamed for the ways I had failed to live lovingly and because of the grief I had caused God, Jesus, and the heavenly beings by my failure." After the review of his life, Storm was told by the angels that he had to go back – that it wasn't his time to die.

And suddenly, the professor found himself back in bed. A surgeon had arrived and his life was saved through an operation. He had been granted a second chance. After months of recuperation back in the U.S., he called that nun he had been so brusque with in his classroom and, weeping, told her what had happened, asking what she thought of it. Did she believe him? Could what he had seen really be true?

The nun's response was that she believed him but wondered what had taken so long: ever since he had made his remarks to her that day in class, she said, she had been praying for him.

Chapter 23

God knows everything that could happen

In his conversations with the angels, Storm says he asked about the nature of God and was told that God knows everything and, more importantly, He knows everything that could happen. From one moment to the next, the Lord knows everything that could occur. From one minute to the next, He is also aware of every possible variable of every event and each outcome. God does not control or dictate the outcome of every event, which would be a violation of His creation, but every living being has its own will that must be expressed. Each conscious being has its own learning to be experienced. God created all things to be what they are and knows that the ultimate outcome is part of His design. Every action serves God's purpose by fulfilling its nature, including the total range of activity, from negative to positive.

Our job is to be positive. Not dwelling on the negative means searching to understand and making sure that we view very situation from the other person's perspective before responding, if another is involved. Is it tough? Very. To slough off agitation, even insult, takes humility.

But it is an absolutely vital component in the spiritual walk and often the results are immediate.

Grace flows to the humble, lubricating the miraculous.

God hears those who have lowered themselves.

"The Lord sustains the humble but casts the wicked to the ground," says *Psalms* 147:6. "He mocks proud mockers but gives grace to the humble," adds *Proverbs* 3:34.

We must always be careful not to judge because when we criticize we are prevented from being children of God. To criticize is to grow in pride. Love, humility, and compassion, on the other hand, conquer evil.

When we humble ourselves, which means to dispel ego, we place God first, and this allows Him room to work. There is even a health benefit: the more humble we are, the more even-tempered we become, and better is the chance we have of softening our arteries (which respond to stress), bolstering our immunity, and lowering our blood pressure.

When I said that hardness of spirit could translate into hardness of heart, I recall the example of a friend's sister. After her husband left her, she took the bitter route, her hatred for him soon growing into a hatred of others – even members of her family.

Her demeanor literally turned hard, expressing itself in a coronary attack that left her with only a quarter of her heart functioning (when she was still only it her thirties). Her heart had grown so hard that it fractured.

Negativity stiffens us and saps our energy while a positive, humble demeanor fortifies us and physically protects us. True, there are people who are born with certain temperaments and find it hard to restrain their emotions. This may be their "cross." But everyone is called to rein in anger, and humility allows us to go outside of ourselves and do just that — at which point we can positively view a circumstance.

When you encounter a person you want to dislike, step back, erase your negative thoughts, and replace them with understanding. If you encounter a person who is slow, exercise patience. If someone insults you, pray for that person. You could be his salvation! And only with prayer do some negative thoughts stop bothering us. It's like God is prompting us to pray for a person through the very aggravation the person has caused!

This takes practice – lots of it — but the most beneficial things are usually the most difficult. *And it's exactly what the Lord wants from us.* If there's a person who rankles you, who you just don't like being around, whom you have antipathy toward, imagine that person as an infant. Reflect on what the person looked like when he or she was a week old, or a month, or as a toddler. *Hold that person in your arms as a child.* You'll see your attitude change. If it's someone close to you who is causing the irritation, reflect on how you would feel if that person were suddenly gone. Mentally embrace those who irk you until it comes easy to you.

If you want to be in tune with God, you have to see as He does and He sees us all as children.

That means if we encounter someone who is rude or awkward, like Dr. Storm, we should reflect on the reason *why* that person may be rude. Might it be something that occurred in childhood? Is he or she suffering unseen physical ailments? Anytime someone is rude, angry, intemperate, insulting, or violent, it grants us the opportunity to pray for that person, which immediately erases the sting from such behavior.

Don't take evil personally. Fight it, resist it, but don't let attacks from the dark side become your obsession. When we respond to the devil, and allow him to engage our emotions, we have opened communication with him. Do you really want to be in touch with the devil?

Now there are times when we have to cite the presence of darkness and are even called to do this. Look at how often Jesus did. Often it takes shedding light on evil to dispel it. We all go through this. When there is suddenly an oppression or atmosphere of argumentation (especially if that rancor is sudden), it can be caused by demons, which seek only to disrupt us, set us off against each other, and rob us of our joy (which means our closeness to God). In some cases, the darkness is attached to a certain person, area, home, room, or even object. Often it comes from books, magazines, or television shows, especially if they involve lewdness or the occult.

These forces must be dispelled or they will block us.

My own return to the Church came because I was rubbing against evil. In my early thirties, I foolishly wrote a book about the Mafia, which exposed me to actual evil. I had to spend time with highly unsavory types, and it rubbed off.

But God took good from this: it is often how He works. He lets us go right to the edge and then rescues us at the last minute (which is why we must always persevere).

Chapter 24

'How could it be raining everywhere but here?'

Evil is best defeated through humility. There's no sting when you have rid yourself of "self." That doesn't mean you're supposed to lose your dignity, or neglect your needs. It means you're to place all of God's needs above yours and the needs of others on a par with your own; such renders evil harmless.

When there is love, faith, and humility, there is actually a "glow" around you. It is the protective bubble. It is the radiation of the Holy Spirit. It envelops those who emulate Christ and forms around their beings like molding on a painting, like a museum's sublime backlighting. Such is represented as a halo.

The more we conform to the desires of Christ, the more glory He sends around us. That comes with a sense of well-being, which is contact through love with God.

With the touch of His favor is also a sharper intuition. *We're more perceptive.* We see with a new clarity. Where sin and evil cloud our ability to choose wisely, holiness leads to wisdom. Where before we saw only a murky picture of the world (if we "saw" anything), we now view the spiritual landscape.

Our spiritual blinders are lifted and the God of signs sends more of them. Call them "signal grace." We get confirmations. This happens when God has responded to humility and the person has been patient with firm faith in the outcome to the end (along with resignation that if it's not in God's Will, it won't happen). We must know how to go with the flow; as *Sirach* says, we should not try to stand against a raging stream; and to do that we have to know where the flow is going (which requires watchfulness).

Important point: we should never want anything too much — except closeness to God.

That's a key test of life, accomplished best through selflessness, which allows us to see straight. Along that path are God's markers to orient us. He is involved with every aspect of our lives and as John Paul II said, "in the designs of Providence there are no mere coincidences." The Lord can work through the subtlety of a conversation or can splash the sky with rainbows, can even skywrite, can exhibit startling specificity. We will never understand how He does it.

A bird will gently totter toward you, a kind stranger will appear, a rainbow will be there on a clear day (and visible during an entire 25-mile trip). I know entire groups that have seen strange "falling" stars. We can say that it's a natural phenomenon, but they come too frequently at certain places of prayer and at poignant times. "We started about 10:00 p.m. praying the Stations of the Cross along the way," says a man named Al Thorrez Jr. of a pilgrimage. " Once we arrived at the Cross, we said some prayers and then looked for a level place to lay our heads about 11:15 p.m. We found a place about forty feet from the Cross to 'set up camp.' The four of us lay down (coincidently in the shape of a cross), and started to pray together as a family holding hands and taking turns thanking God and presenting petitions and then concluding with the *Our Father* and *Hail Mary*. While I was thanking God, I saw a very vibrant shooting star and paused briefly to see what would happen to the 'star.' After we finished our family prayer, I explained why I paused during the prayer and all my family had seen the shooting star, too. A few seconds later, we saw another shooting star. My younger son, Clayton, started counting them. I had actually seen one earlier in the night. Without going into loads of detail, it was tough to close our eyes and get some sleep because we kept seeing shooting stars. I counted over thirty shooting stars while my younger son counted 22 (he also said he twice saw two simultaneous shooting stars). About three a.m. I opened my eyes and saw light emanating behind the Cross. As I leaned forward to see where the light was coming from, I beheld a double crescent moon. I took some pictures which look very similar to what I saw with my naked eye."

These are actual accounts I have collected.

From Malayasia. From Tobanga.

Birds will circle with joyous calls.

License plates? "I was going through a horrid period of self condemnation, unforgiveness, and depression for events that had happened in my life," said a woman named Celeste Taylor. "I was not close to God in any way. I did not go to church. I was driving on the southern California freeway and talking to myself about how worthless my life seemed and questioning whether my existence even mattered! It was a major low point in my life. I will never forget the brown Mercedes SL that came up from behind and swooshed past me on the road. Before it was out of sight I had gotten a chance to see the license plate 'URFRGVN'".

I heard from another woman who was striving to do her best but was exasperated. Nothing was going right. "I was on my way home from work and was complaining to God about the state of my spiritual life for about 15 minutes, just going on and on," she says. "I was telling God about how hard I was trying and I wasn't seeing any progress. I was getting more and more distraught and frustrated and finally yelled at Him like a spoiled child having a tantrum, 'What is it that you want from me? What is it that I need to say to you? What are the words that you want to hear?' With that a car pulled in front of me with a license plate that read, 'YESGOD.'"

He wants us to say yes to all the tests.

Another was beside herself with the work of a mother. Her young children were demanding all of her time. She finally found a moment to stop and watch a religious video — which discussed a sign that had come in the form of roses.

This was in response to a saint's exasperation over trivial daily chores. The young mother was feeling the same way. When her son interrupted, wanting her to play with him on the computer (he was too young to do it alone), they went to the computer and the desktop sprang to life — with gorgeous roses. "I truly believe that God spoke clearly to me that day about the immense meaning and significance of our daily duties, particularly those acts that aren't written about in saint books, like playing a game with our children when we'd rather be watching a video, or reading a magazine," she noted.

Seeing straight is seeing the big in the small.

Did I say "skywriting"? "After several weeks of bad business I was worried about how I was going to meet expenses in our store," said Jo Kuczenski of Boca Raton. "I pray the Rosary to and from work every day, but this day I was very worried and asked for a sign that all would be well. As I parked my vehicle and walked to the storefront, right above our building was the skywriter and he wrote 'Trust Jesus.' I needed nothing more and the sales that day were outstanding."

I know of a nun who had searched years to find the right place for a retreat center and ended up locating a parcel that precisely fit a vision given to a friend years before. When they took that there, she found a rock eroded in a pattern that looked like Jesus!

It should come as no surprise that there are so many reports of images that look like Jesus, Mary, or one of the saints formed in stones, trees, clouds, or the reflections of windows. Some of these images are barely discernible (and open to dispute, such as the Blessed Mother in a cheese sandwich), but others are so striking as to void the argument of "chance." Images have appeared in trees in Salt Lake City and even Manhattan just before September 11. In California, several small hamlets of Mexican immigrants have report luminous crosses that appear on windows. At first one would write this off to reflections from internal light, and even chicanery, but witnesses have described more than just a single luminous formation (they saw additional images *inside* the crosses), and asserted that the crosses were visible even when the interior lights were out.

This particular phenomenon began on Ash Wednesday in 2002 when a man named Jesus Aceva in the town of Thermal near Riverside was checking out his yard and noticed something mysterious. A beam of light seemed to flare from above and then "inflect" itself onto the glass of the door to his home – a description that, if accurate, is not explicable.

According to daughter Perla, Aceva at first was afraid to tell anyone and slipped back into bed. But it was impossible to sleep, having seen what he just had seen, and Aceva got up, woke the others, and they all went outside to see it: a luminous cross on the door, one that remained for years after.

Skeptics said they were simple reflections on glass while believers described a conviction that the "reflections" (which spread to other homes) had an extra dimension to them.

This was also true of the way oxidation formed a large, striking image of the Blessed Mother on the glass of an office building in Clearwater, Florida. The image, which first appeared in 1996, perfectly fit the proportions of the famous Virgin of Guadalupe, with similar coloration spanning nine separate panes of glass (which made it hard to dismiss as mere happenstance!). Most often, God does not part the Red Sea; He works within the normal course of nature. In this case it was oxidation.

This raises an important point: just because we can explain the process by which something formed *does not negate the fact that it was God Who formed it using that process.*

Sap on a tree congeals to look like the Madonna or the bark peals away in the pattern of Jesus' face, or a cross; an icicle is a dead-ringer for Mary.

Visiting the peasant hinterlands of Ukraine shortly after the fall of Communism, I was shown an image that had suddenly appeared on a pane of glass at a home south of a village called Buchach. In this case it was not oxidation; it was etched. At first wary, and sending me on a wild goose chase (it had been hidden away from the Communists), the villagers eventually brought the pane of glass out, carefully unwrapped it, and let me see it.

And there I was, gazing at what looked like the detailed outline of a bearded man that seemed etched into the glass but *wasn't*. It was just there (along with an indescribable feeling).

These are all ways by which God communicates to and blesses us at special moments.

Always be aware of what is transpiring around you.

God invented the laws of physics. There is constant play between the natural and supernatural.

I have seen extraordinary photos of the aurora borealis, including one that showed what seemed to be the image of a huge descending angel over Scandinavia around 9/11.

Likewise, galaxies photographed through new and powerful telescopes often contain "hidden" images.

The God of miracles is a God Who can reach the tiniest and most gargantuan places with identical ease.

In Canada, frost may form into a perfect cross, the sun may reflect strangely, or there may be incredibly detailed images in rose petals down in the Philippines.

Frequent are the reports of unusual clouds at strategic moments.

"In July 2004, some members of my family went for a picnic at a park," said an Iowa woman, Anne Elizabeth. "When we were eating our lunch and gazing at the beautiful scenery, my mom noticed a rainbow in the middle of a cloud in the sky. It was not rainy, but even rather sunny that day, as I remember. My father, two sisters, and I marveled at this unusual occurrence, and my parents commented that it must be a sign from God that 'everything would be all right.'" Little did they know that a brother had died that afternoon, around that very time.

While skeptics scoff at this — pointing out that all kinds of things can be imagined in the sky, which, to a point, is true (it's called "pareidolia") — there are cases that remain beyond the bounds of explanation.

Tom Rutkoski of Evans City, Pennsylvania, related one that occurred on August 5, 1991.

"It was in response to a request I made of the Lord," wrote Rutkoski, a former television-news cameraman, who was ready to become a lay minister but wanted confirmation. "*'If this is really You, Lord, working in my life, I would like a sign in the sky that I can photograph,'* [I had prayed]. I was asking for a confirmation because I wanted to give my whole life to Jesus.

Rutkoski says it came in the way of a cloud that contained the shape of a cross and symbols of the Blessed Mother as well as the Father, Son, and Holy Spirit.

Others independently witnessed the same cloud and, later, the formation reappeared in the sky at places where Rutkoski went to preach. In 1996, before one of his talks on Long Island, a Nigerian priest was shocked to see the same cloud formation.

It was also witnessed by a couple after a talk Tom gave in Vermont.

"This image has followed me around the world as I go evangelizing," says Rutkoski. "People tell me, from time to time, about a very definite cloud shape that appeared over their towns before, during, or after my visit." On one occasion, when rain was predicted to wash out a planned retreat, Rutkoski vowed to the weatherman at the TV station where he worked that "the power of God" would halt the rain. The meteorologist laughed (the prediction was that it was going to rain hard all day, a virtually hundred-percent chance) and, indeed, when Rutkoski peered out that morning, it was raining miserably.

"I looked up into the sky and spoke to God," he recalled. "'Hey, God, You said if I wanted to move a mountain, I could, if I had enough faith. So I ask You, with the faith You taught me to have, please stop this rain, part these skies, and bring the sun out. There are six hundred people coming here to pray and they will not come if it is raining. Oh, and if You are going to do this, You will also need to bring a lot of wind because the road is all mud now and people will not be able to drive on the road to get to this farm.'

Recounted Rutkoski:

"*That moment the rain ceased.* The clouds rolled back, and the sun came out. And then the wind began to blow.

"In one hour the road was dry and people from all around the area came to our farm to pray.

"They all had the same words on their lips: '*How could it be raining everywhere but here?*'"

Chapter 25

The light through the window

Those are the events we read about, but we are all privy to more subtle miracles. Just as the good Lord can cause a candle to drip in just such a way as to resemble an angel, or the sun to reflect just a bit unusually, or bark on a tree to form into what looks like a vague silhouette of Jesus, so too does He tweak and manipulate everyday events in such a way that timing goes just right for us and we cook with exactly the right ingredients and there are other favorable events that let us know He is there without some sort of spectacular show of fire from the sky. God is subtle with His wonders because He always wants to leave room for faith. Look for miracles in the ordinary. See God always and everywhere. Look for the signs that flow with your daily routine and accept the course of events as directed. Remember that when it is God's timing, *there is never frenzy.*

Give yourself to Him from the top of your head to the bottom of your toes and the way is set for Him to control the flow. Don't strive for control yourself. That's for the intellectuals. Always leave room for God to work. "I will destroy the wisdom of the wise, and the learning of the learned I will set aside," says *1 Corinthians* 1. Christ chooses the humble. Those with humility have lowered themselves so they can exalt God.

In other words, when we try to inject ourselves and our pretensions into our reality, we accomplish the opposite of what we're looking to accomplish. Keep it simple. Don't replace humble spirituality with high-flying theological language. Jesus did not wander the countryside with a blackboard, did not cite bylaws, and did not speak in polysyllables (that was for the Pharisees). It's simplicity that leads to direct communication. Simple requests work wonders, connecting us in a direct way with God, Who especially answers our prayers for children. I know a Catholic radio broadcaster, Barbaranne Marion, in Pennsylvania, and one Christmas she and her husband couldn't afford gifts for their children – who were anxiously awaiting Santa. Settling herself down, she prayed for the Blessed Mother to hear her – *really* prayed. "I wanted nothing for myself," she said. "Just for the kids." How could they be left without gifts? How could she possibly face such disappointment? She did not. The very next day her husband John went to get the mail and found one envelope that had been stuffed in there by hand, without postage. It was from a wealthy listener who said she felt "told" by the Blessed Virgin to give the Marions $1,500 (the check was enclosed) to be used solely "for the joys of Christmas." That's how directly God can work, if we think He can work that way.

On the other hand, our best efforts can be frustrated when we're operating in selfishness. When things don't "go right," when we're "all thumbs," when it's "just not our day," God may be throwing us a hint.

Say you're on the way to the store and all the way you run into frustrating traffic; once you're there, the clerk is rude; he doesn't have the right brand of cigarettes (or let's say it's liquor); once you do buy something and return, the package rolls off the seat. Could God be telling you something about liquor?

Imagine reaching for it, which could cause a distraction and perhaps even a minor accident. This too would be in keeping with God's way. And this too is a sign. *God usually sends little fender- benders in an effort to prevent major accidents.* When He pierces us, we lose our puffiness. Suffering causes humility. He tries to get us to shift course if we're straying in a way that could be harmful. And so such a nudge is also a miracle.

Are you frustrated in your search for a job because you're looking for the wrong kind of work? Are you butting your head against a wall because you are self-seeking, materialistic, or overly ambitious? Are you seeking to imitate the gifts of another instead of utilizing what God has given you?

If so, expect counter-miracles.

That's not to say that every misfortune is a sign that God is displeased. We can be in step with God – doing His Will — and face similar challenges. Such are the "tests" of life. As I mentioned, there is resistance from the enemy. But during runs of bad luck, we should pray to discern a pattern. If what we are trying to do is His Will, in the end what we are pursuing will succeed and will do so in proportion to our faith, as well as our diligence. In those cases, the Lord steers our way. In the storm, we are protected.

On the other hand, when we're out of step with God, it can be not only frustrating, but dangerous. The Lord has our eternity in mind and will allow events to reorient us. As it says in Scripture (*Sirach* 20:8), "some misfortunes bring success." Look at Howard Storm (or I should say, Reverend Storm).

In other cases, as opposed to altering our course, we are receiving simple warnings.

"I looked up, and there was a truck coming in the other direction," said actor Mel Gibson of a close brush with death. "The last thing I remember before I simply just covered up in a crouch position, let go of the steering wheel, and put it in the hands of the Almighty was a massive gum tree coming right at me just before it went down over the cliff. And I felt this bang, boom, bang, like this. I took my hands off, and the car was ok. The big gum tree was pressed against one side of the car door, and it had dented it in. And on the other side of the car was a sapling. I had been caught between the two trees, and the front wheels were hanging over the abyss. Somebody had His Hand on me that day. And I figure it's things like that that kind of inform you of something greater than yourself perhaps watching over you."

In 2005, a first-time skydiver survived a 3,500-foot plunge to earth after his parachute failed to open properly. He told a national television audience that he experienced extraordinary comfort as he prayed on the way down. He said he made a last-minute plea to God. "I said, 'OK, well, I trust you, I believe in you, and if there's any way, I'd love to see my family again, so help me out here,'" recounted the man, Daniel Levy Cave, who was skydiving near Seattle. "And I just felt — I got to say, I just felt like the biggest hug in the world and just this warm embrace. It was the most amazing thing ever. And at that point, I thought, either way, this is going to turn out good, so, and here I am. I don't know how." He came away with only a broken leg, a broken jaw, and some internal injuries. That's more than twice the height of the Empire State Building.

A hand saves a woman as she is ready to go over the brink of the Niagara. It is a human hand. But who put that person there?

When we have accidents (or close calls), we have to pay attention to what God may be saying. He may not be saying anything we can immediately discern. There are cycles in life. There are misfortunes programmed into our lives to strengthen us. Events occur to draw us closer to God. There are also attacks from the dark side – from the fallen angels who seek to impede our progress. In fact, such events may increase *as we draw closer to the Lord.*

But more often than not, events have meaning; and more often than not, we don't see it. Life is a tapestry and from earth we see only the underside of it. But events weave one into another. Depending on our response, we progress or stay where we are. Joe Whalen from Quincy, Massachusetts, was a knock-down, drag-out alcoholic much of his life – to the point where he lost his job and was divorced by his wife after decades of marriage. So depressed was he that he prayed he'd get cancer. But he went to see a priest, and during that visit, he made an honest Confession.

That simple action led to a flurry of the miraculous.

In this case the first manifestation was visions.

"After prayers, with my eyes closed but before going to sleep, I would first see pinpoints of light, then whole fields of brilliant bluish light, pulsating like a kaleidoscope," he related. "They continued every night for seven months. Sometimes I would see Jesus suspended from the Cross, one heart with two circlets of thorns around it, or two hearts with thorns around them. Many times I would see a big white dove heading toward me as the field of vision became an intense blue-white. In the last vision I saw two angels suspended with their wings fluttering and a dove gliding toward them."

The visions were not without significance; they made such a profound impression that Whalen ended up applying for the seminary and became a priest at 69 — not only a priest, but one who was soon in a miraculous healing ministry!

Mostly God nudges us less dramatically. He may allow us to take ill with a cold or the flu when we need recollection. This is a gift. He may withdraw money so we have to stay home and read. Praise Him for that. He may allow a health scare to teach us to pray. *Tribulation puts things in perspective.*

And the greater the tribulation, the more opportunity there is for the miraculous. I know a man named Louis Saia who was going crazy because a large company had allegedly "stolen" an idea from him and stripped him of a small fortune. The tension of a court battle with this powerful corporation was ripping up his finances, his emotions, and his marriage – to the point where he was on sedatives. Endlessly pacing, Louis literally wore a pattern into a wooden kitchen floor! But one day, trying to jog off the tension (at wit's end — like Father Whalen, no longer caring if he lived or died), he spotted what appeared to be an apparitional woman at the door of a building he had used as an office. Mesmerized, he stared at a short female attired as if from ancient Jerusalem. When Saia drew closer, he noticed he could see through her — she was translucent — and while he could still discern the linen, it was not of this world, but more like a "liquid." She was an ethereal presence – and all she said was, *"Have faith in my Son Jesus."*

Those words saved Louis' life and he went on to a dramatic, improbable victory against the corporation.

"All these Harvard lawyers and Yale lawyers made my problem so complex with the business situation, and she solves the business situation but more importantly the situation of losing my life, saved me from dying from stress, and also saved my eternal life with one sentence: *Just have faith in my Son Jesus,"* Louis told me. "I trusted. It was out of my hands from that day forward. All I did was pray."

Faith had turned into trust. Trust had graduated into surrender.

And what happened was astounding. His lawyers had abandoned him. Banks wouldn't lend him money. His own family wouldn't give him any more funds for his case (it seemed so hopeless). But Louis persevered. He had invented a valuable product — a shipping container — that the corporation wanted to assume total control over, and he couldn't accept that. He couldn't accept someone taking away his invention, his great accomplishment, his life's work, in his reckoning of the battle, and so he persevered and trusted and right after the vision — within days — two new lawyers showed up, agreeing to work on a contingency basis. Still, Saia was in desperate need of money, and that was where a second miracle took place. The same week, a man from Volvo Credit came to see him for a previously scheduled meeting (one that Saia had all but forgotten) and now Louis poured his heart out to this man, telling him of his financial desperation and the appearance of Mary (despite the fact that the executive was Protestant).

The story took three hours to tell and at the end the executive told Louis that his sob story and poor credit risk were hardly the basis on which to loan him what he needed (five million). But he startled Saia by adding that he *believed Louis would win the case and that he would lend the money based on the story.*

It turned out that the executive was deeply religious.

Saia and his wife wondered if he was joking, but the next day came a fax confirming the loan and talking about Jesus.

Louis went on the win the court case, and at the most crucial moment in the courtroom, a beam of light streamed through the window and reflected on a suddenly favorable judge.

Chapter 26

Magnify and multiply

As the saying goes, the darkest moment is just before dawn unless we hold onto the darkness.

Tribulation should lead to new ways of viewing life, and that leads to joy, the emotion of miracles, along with love (which *causes* joy). God is love. God is joy. There you have the key to life. Difficulty opens us to love.

And so, handled well, suffering leads to resurrection.

When we don't recognize our faults (during a disturbance in our lives) — when we don't get down on our knees, and stay there, repenting and looking to Jesus — the problems grow larger.

Those who get legalistic lack miracles because they become so immersed in the minutiae or mechanics of religion that the earth they till is hard.

Don't confuse "religious" with "spiritual." Religion is a discipline that is supposed to lead to spirituality, but frequently it doesn't. Too often, it becomes the subject of idolatry. We focus on the religion, the institution, instead of the Holy Spirit, when what we are called to is contact through love with God.

We have to *ardently,* directly seek God and the more direct we are with Him, the quicker He responds. Use the discipline of religion to love. He wants us to communicate (during Communion) from the heart.

Think of times when you have been in crisis, you've been desperate, the darkest moments. How did you pray then? If your requests poured from your being, if you prayed from the bottom of your soul, and if you felt a surrender, then you prayed with your heart. You did it!

If you could pray that way every time, you'd be loaded with miracles.

With prayer from the heart there is a new openness to God and even the environment responds around us (see "green thumb"). Any miracle is possible.

In conformance with Christ, we prosper. He can make something from nothing.

I don't think there's a better example than the poor people of Juarez,

Mexico.

Many of them are what they call "trash grubbers," and live near the U.S. border. Surviving on what they find at a local dump, they live in vast barrios with no electricity, sanitation, or running water. There is no such thing as welfare. They don't need it. They are recipients of miracles right out of the Bible. It started back in Christmas of 1972 when a charismatic prayer group led by a Jesuit priest named Father Richard Thomas decided to prepare dinner for the indigents. From 11 a.m. until late afternoon, they did just that, organizing a charitable meal — and there was plenty of it. Everyone received a generous share. In fact, there was food leftover. What was unusual is that *everyone* ate although Father Thomas and his group had prepared ham for only 150 people — not the 300 who came and even had seconds.

Those cutting the meat felt as if it was not diminishing even as they sliced off portions.

It seemed to stay the same size. There was enough left over for people to take it home with them! *It seemed to multiply*. Time and again, this would happen when Father Thomas and his group were ministering to the poor. They also fed those in prison. Fruit. Bread. All seemed to be in endless supply at special dinners, despite heaping portions. When a woman named Carole Raymond was preparing a mixture of flour to make tortillas, she was astonished at how the sack stayed the same size. In one case, each of 500 people was given a can of milk even though they started with just 350 cans.

The same happened with squash, grapes, and avocados.

It was the phenomenon of "multiplication" and like the unfolding of a bud, it occurred almost imperceptibly, said Father Thomas. On one occasion he was aware of the multiplication as it was actually occurring. "We were visiting the jail," the priest said. "It was the week before Easter and we were giving the prisoners a special Mexican dish of bread pudding and as we were spooning it out, the lady told me there wouldn't be enough because they let prisoners out of cells that held 75 or 80 of them."

Dozens more than expected.

Yet everybody had a paper plate heaped up with food, and they were also given more lemonade than the group had brought. The prisoners got all the lemonade they wanted. This went on for half an hour. "We all realized what was happening," said the priest. The supply of lemonade held even though the woman in charge of it already had tipped the container over to eke out the final three or four cups – dozens of cups before it actually ended. "We could see there was no end to the lemonade she could get out," he said. "Then we gave it to all the police and guards — all they wanted, more than we planned. After no one wanted any more, there was no more left."

God multiplies in all our lives but does so in a way that seems so natural that we take it for just that. Almost everyone has known times when just the right money came when money was tight or when the bank account seemed larger than expected.

When God is close, there is all we need. This also occurred to Bob Rice, the former truck driver who reported healings. Serving as a Eucharistic minister during a visit to a church in Damascus, Maryland, he watched in disbelief as drops of wine appeared one after another at the bottom of a chalice when congregants continued to line up for the Precious Blood — even though the wine had run out when a young man "chug-a-lugged" all of it. "Every person who wanted to receive the Precious Blood was able to receive it," he noted with awe.

This goes to *Hebrews* 11:3, which informs us that "through faith we perceive that the worlds were created by the word of God, and that what is visible came into being through the invisible."

When we choose to serve Him – when we glory in Him – *anything can happen*. He draws close and brings forth from nothingness. He multiplies what is necessary for us to serve and suddenly finances may go our way or there are friends when we need friends. Things come out of the "blue."

In Scripture, the Lord sent *manna* and even caused water to come from a rock, which also occurred in the 18th century with a missionary named Father Magin Catala. On one occasion the priest, who ministered in the thirsting, desert terrain of the Santa Clara Valley, told his companions to look for water under a particular rock he described and they were astonished to find it. When they returned later, the water and rock were both inexplicably gone.

Father Magin had a faith like Moses, who "Looked unto the reward," "for he endured as seeing Him that is invisible" (*Hebrews* 10: 26, 27).

Chapter 27

There is no situation from which God is absent

God loves it when we can fly above a disappointment, sorrow, or tragedy and find His comfort. If you want Him to multiply what you need, send Him the ingredient of enthusiasm and refuse to immerse yourself in setbacks, however big or small. A second widow of 9/11, Cheryl McGuinness, whose husband was the pilot of a plane that hit the Trade Center, says she wants other people to realize that no matter what disasters or pain occur in life ("no matter how horrific they can be"), those tragedies can be overcome by "having a foundation that we can draw on in times of tragedy and trial."

That foundation is seeing the Hand of God in everything, which then makes it easier for us to put everything into His Hands. Let's repeat it: *seeing the Hand of God in everything makes it easier to put everything in His Hands.*

God has His reasons and He reaches everywhere, if we avail ourselves. He always gives us options, and one of them is to draw near to Him, in which case He will meet us at least halfway and comfort us no matter how dire the situation. He always rewards us in a way that exceeds what we deserve and keeps close track of our good qualities. *There is no situation from which He is absent.* And although it may look like it to us, He is never random.

All day every day, He is tweaking our cells to function properly, to avoid disease, when it is His Will, when we are in tune with the health of His Spirit, and this should give us tremendous hope: the knowledge that we are not vulnerable to the capricious forces of nature – to bad genes, to carcinogens, to arteriosclerosis – when God is allowed to permeate every part of our beings. When huge events occur, He may send emissaries.

Ask a Florida man named Stan Rutherford, who once detested religion. That bitterness came from foster homes and abuse; anyone reading his life story would sympathize with why he turned out the way he did. Although raised Pentecostal, by adulthood Stan, a drug user who did jail time, couldn't stand the Name of Jesus. Cocaine was his god; he would snort a line of it in the morning – "before my feet even hit the ground."

But all that changed in 1991. It started when a neighbor ran across him one day and told Stan that God had given her a prophetic "word" about him during a prayer meeting.

"She told me if I didn't change my ways by the time I was 45 years old, that the Lord would pull His grace of mercy off me," relates Rutherford. "It sort of stuck with me that someone would say that, because normally if you came in my face about religion, I'd slap you! I just hated anybody who had anything to do with God — period. But for some reason I listened to this lady."

The fateful day turned out to be November 4, 1991. He had just started a job supervising a crew that scoured large phosphate tanks near Lakeland, Florida, and on the way to work, there was a foreboding — "like this black cloud, this terrible feeling like I was going to die," Rutherford recalls.

"I even called my wife and told her that if I didn't see her any more, I loved her, that she was the only woman I ever really loved," he says.

Stan and his crew went up to the mines at about 7 a.m., and shortly after, by quarter to eight, "all hell" broke loose.

When Stan returned to one of the tanks after checking a crew, someone gave a signal to the mechanic and the mechanic kicked the high-pressure machine on, creating 3,500 pounds per square inch of laser-like water.

"The custom was to chain it down to keep it in place," he recalls. "But they didn't chain it down. They tied it in place with a rope. And it broke loose. Now, realize that it takes eight men just to hold that hose at 3,500 pounds!"

A hose spewing a "laser" of water was dancing a dance of death. At that pressure, the water creates heat as it comes out of the nozzle. As Rutherford tried to save a man trapped on scaffolding, the jet of water slashed his left side and cut through him, ripping near a kidney and coming out three inches away. It was literally tearing through him. "It didn't just hit me once. It hit me three times and kept cutting into me. It blew me up against the wall with such force that it cracked my safety helmet," Stan said of the horrid experience. "Somebody reached in and grabbed me by the foot and yanked me out. I was sitting there with my clothes ripped off and didn't know I was that hurt. But then one of the men said, 'My God, Mr. Stan, I can see your guts!'"

Rutherford was rushed to a clinic where a company doctor insisted that Stan would be okay. Three days after, however, Stan felt like he was having a heart attack. One of his legs turned black. An x-ray showed that huge quantities of phosphate had been blown into his organs. He was rushed to a hospital, this time knowing that he was injured seriously.

Doctors were afraid to operate. It would put him in great peril. He was in no shape for it. But they had no choice. "I had like thirty pounds of filth and excess fluid in my body," recalls the Florida man.

"I went in for the surgery and they gave me a shot and I was out," he recalls. "But what they told us later was that I had 'died,' that I had awakened during the procedure and they tried to re-sedate me and I died."

Does God really wait until the last minute?

He can go *beyond* the last minute.

It was at this point – in a hospital room for those who had expired, ready for the morgue, considered gone by his doctors — that God intervened and Stan Rutherford somehow regained consciousness. "This little nun came and touched me on the face, tapped me on the face, and said, *'Wake up. We have work for you to do!'*" says Rutherford – up to then ardently anti-Catholic. "I guess I saw her in the state of being unconscious. I don't know how to explain it, but when I woke up there was this little woman dressed in white and a kind of turquoise blue robe — this little beautiful nun with these exquisite eyes. You had to see her eyes!"

A moment later, she was gone.

Chapter 28

Remember that God often waits until the last moment

God waits until the last second and at times beyond the last second, because He knows precisely where we are (in relation to the eternal) and is in total control of all forces around us. Rutherford was left for dead, but God had other plans. Stan had tried to save another person, and despite his own anti-religious life, that was enough for God to give him a second chance.

He too is now an evangelist. Can you imagine what would have occurred if he had gone back to his old ways?

There are many who report instances of mysterious strangers. Who are they? How does God orchestrate this? Have there been mysterious strangers in our own lives (heed *Hebrews* 13:2)?

In Stan's case, it was the Blessed Mother; other times, they are angels. Such spirits coordinate the miraculous as God's agents and can appear anywhere in any form. As spirits, they exist on a different level of energy, but can vibrate down to ours. I know of instances where a strange-looking plow suddenly appeared when a woman was struggling to dig herself out of a snowstorm, or where a tow truck arrives to help a stranded car driver (in one case, displaying God's sense of humor, with the words "Heavenly Towing" on a side door). Joann Farrell in Yorktown Heights, New York, recounted the time her husband had just come out of heart surgery and her kids had moved to New York City, leaving her with sole snow-removal duties.

Neighbors helped, but one day, in March of 1996, it was just too much. Out there in the driveway, trying to grapple with a major storm, Joann broke down in tears.

"As I took a break, with tears running down my face, I was thinking that I will never be able to shovel out the mound the town plow had left across the bottom of the driveway," she said. "As I stood there looking at all I still had to do, I saw headlights coming from a few blocks away. They turned up my road and as they came closer I could see it was a pickup truck with a plow on the front. I thought to myself, 'boy, someone is lucky to have that truck coming to them.'

"Well, that truck went past all the other houses and came right to my driveway and cleared snow that was blocking the whole bottom of my driveway! It then went up to the corner, came back down, and plowed more across the bottom. I was so shocked I just stood leaning on my shovel looking at 'them.' There were two men in the truck, one with the 'whitest' hair, who was driving, and one with stark black hair sitting in the passenger seat. When they finished clearing the bottom of the driveway, they backed up a little, both looked at me and smiled, waved, and then drove away. I never approached them or spoke to them, as I seemed to be rooted to my spot. As I watched them drive away, I noticed that the truck was solid white with no commercial writing on it. It was a strange truck as the back almost looked more like a boat than a truck. I had never seen that truck before, nor have I seen it since. In the 27 years I have been a homeowner I have never had anyone come and plow my driveway out like that. I felt very peaceful, and an overwhelming feeling that I was not alone settled over me."

Of course, when those who are assisted attempt to track down their help (such as the towing company), there is no such listing. For the most part, they are invisible agents that we do well to invoke, in the Name of Jesus, when we need a miracle.

Angels surround us. We can call on an army of them. They delight in our requests. They are underutilized. And they can be invoked at the highest ranks, especially in times of stress.

When we die and are shown our lives, we'll be astonished at how many times angels intervened for us, and at how many times "strangers" we brushed by and forgot were actually agents of God in human form.

All of us have encountered them, and some of the brushes are more apparent than others. Such was the case with a woman from Seattle named Kimberly, who had her encounter during a trip to Hawaii. Body surfing with her fiancé, they were caught in a sudden rip current. She got back, but her boyfriend was swept out, along with two others, under huge waves.

This woman – who like Stan had a previous near-death episode – prayed with fervent faith. Was it the experience that enabled her? She asked for the angels. Desperately! As she did, a sort of tunnel opened, and in the next moment, she saw two objects heading through the waves for her fiancé.

They were "surfers" who plucked out the struggling men.

They dragged first one man, then another, across their boards and got them back to the beach.

Kimberly was wrapping towels around the shivering men who had been rescued when suddenly "a heavyset Hawaiian woman appeared, striding purposefully out of the jungle beside the beach," she recounted. "She wore a faded sarong and had thick black hair hung in a shank down her back. She wasn't just large, she was massive, and when she padded across the sand in her rubber-soled thongs, I swear the earth shook. Her face was impassive as she headed straight for Don, who stood up at her approach.

"Slowly, she lifted her two brown arms, placed her hands on Don's shoulders, looked deep into his eyes, and said, 'You lucky, man. No surf-boarders, you dead. You lucky, man.' Her pronouncement concluded, she regally walked back into the jungle, while we watched in open-mouthed amazement." When Kimberly, her fiancé, and the others turned to thank the surfers, who could have not left the vicinity without being seen doing so, there was no one there.

When we need help and have been faithful to God, when we pray from the heart, and especially when we are desperate, God responds.

As difficult as it is for us to understand, angels can "precipitate" into our realm and take whatever form is necessary. I have seen accounts of them rescuing those in medical need, or even appearing at the scene to help put out a fire. Take the case of Karen Spruck from Hawthorne, New York, who was with her family traveling in a van on the New York State Thruway when suddenly they were passed by two unusual-looking men who were urgently signaling to them to pull over.

At the same time, all of the signals on their dashboard were going haywire. The engine stopped. Something was wrong.

They were warning her; the van was blazing with fire.

Quickly the Sprucks pulled over and piled out in a mad dash but found to their horror that they were unable to pull out their five-year-old daughter.

"The flames were coming out from under the van as I was trying to get out," Karen said. "As I was struggling to get her out, the two men had stomped on the fire and were spraying fire extinguishers. They kept the fire under control while I finally got my daughter out. There was a state fair in the area on this weekend so the fire engines came quickly. After I got my daughter out and after they had the fire out I didn't see the first two men. I wanted to thank them because I hate to think of what would have happened if they hadn't kept the fire under control. When I asked the firemen where the two men with the fire extinguishers went, *they said there had been no one else there.*"

Wrote another witness: "Such an event happened to me many years ago when my first son was only six weeks old. Some friends of ours graciously volunteered to watch our baby for a much needed night out to the movies. When we got back I went upstairs to get my baby boy. I laid him over my shoulder and started down the stairs. I had high heels on at the time, the fashionable thing to do. When I stepped down to the first step I tripped and proceeded to fall down the stairs with my baby over my shoulder. These were very steep stairs made out of wood with no carpeting. There was a guard rail on the right side, and the wall on the left. I couldn't grab the guard rail because that's the shoulder I had my baby over. So I proceeded to fall from the very top to the very bottom of that staircase. The thought of it to me now is truly amazing. I never bumped into anything, or even touched the wall or the stairs. I just remember knowing I had to turn over and land on my back at the bottom of the stairs, which also had no carpet. I turned around in midair and landed on my back on the bottom of the stairs, with my baby on his back over my stomach. I had no injuries whatsoever from my fall, and neither did my baby. There were no bruises, or any aches or pains. I was relieved my baby was all right, and I got up and walked out. My husband and friends could not believe what happened. I really didn't think much about it at the time. It wasn't until years later that I realized what exactly did happen. When I started to fall, it was like I was carried down the stairs, or floated down on a cloud. I was falling down head first and miraculously did not bump into anything. Before I reached the bottom I turned over to save my baby. There was no way that was humanly possible. I see my son today, he's thirty-five, and his four children and thank God for those angels He sent to me that night. I'm sure it was my guardian angel, or angels, that carried me down those stairs, enfolding me in their protective presence."

The Bible tells us that "He will give His angels charge concerning you, to guard you in all your ways [*Psalms* 91:11]. "On their hands they will bear you up," adds *Matthew* 4:6, "so that you will not strike your foot against a stone."

Father Donald Guglielmi of St. Mark's Church in Stratford, Connecticut, noted:

"On April 11, 2003 I was driving home on I-91 South around noon in Connecticut in a heavy rain and heavy traffic. I was doing about 70 miles per hour and was traveling in the far left lane. All of a sudden, my car tires hit a large pool of water and my car spun totally out of control. The car swerved into the middle lane and spun around two or three times. I could not control these movements and could see traffic heading towards me and all around me. I remember bracing myself for a collision — that never came. Instead, the car spun all the way over to the far right hand lane and hit the embankment, where it came to a dead stop, facing the same direction I had been driving in! I was shaken, but uninjured and there was not even a scratch on my car. It was then I realized that I had been praying the Chaplet of Divine Mercy at the time of this incident. I sensed immediately that the angels of God had intervened and prevented what could have easily been a fatal accident. There appears to be no other explanation since the highway was filled with speeding cars and the chance of spinning into the middle lanes without hitting another vehicle seemed impossible at the time."

When our prayers are sincere, and especially when our prayers are for others – with the energy of desperation — they go up like beams of light and are answered as long as they do not interfere with God's plan or the free will of another. The angels know us by name and our prayers excite them into action. We can be desperate – fervent – without really being "desperate."

Angels are especially prone to those who work for the Lord, such as Barry Hoare of Cairns in Queensland, Australia. "In 1963 my wife and I went to work as lay-missionaries in the Vicariate of Wewak in Papua New Guinea," he says. "We were posted to a mission station at 'Roma' in the Sepik River Area with an Irish priest, Father Patrick Hallinan. On many weekends my wife and I would walk to nearby mission stations to visit with the mission priest or nuns.

"On one particular weekend we went to a mission at Ulupu — some four and a half hours walk — into the hills to visit with a priest named Father Knorr. We had lunch with father, listened to some of his stories, and spent the afternoon with him.

That evening, they headed home.

"We had a torch to help show the way as night progressed," said Barry. Not long after leaving the mission station and walking downhill for some time, they crossed a small river and soon a thunderstorm struck. It was totally dark and the missionary took a torch out of his haversack.

With the rain pouring on it, however, the torch gave a couple of flickers and went out, leaving them in complete darkness.

"Going back was not an option because the small river would have become a raging torrent," said Hoare. "While wondering what the best thing to do would be, I suddenly noticed something burning on the top of a hill about 150 meters in front of us — *a very bright light in the darkness.* We began walking towards it and while doing so the rain stopped.

"The light remained and we soon came across a native man holding a lighted *'boom boom'* — a palm branch from the coconut tree, which gives very good light and burns for maybe three or four minutes.

"He spoke to us in pigin English: *'yu pela go wer'* ('where are you two going'). We answered that we were going to the mission station of Roma. He then told us in pigin that he would take us on a short cut and we set off following him and the lighted palm branch into the jungle — up and down some hills and across some small creeks and within what seemed a very short time we came out at the village of Saigisi, about half an hour from home."

The storm clouds had disappeared and it was now a moonlit sky. The whole journey, which had taken the missionary and his wife four and a half hours on the way to *Ulupu,* was completed in an *hour.* Moreover, the guide never changed the *boom-boom* and yet it never went out.

Perhaps most extraordinary is when angels leave something behind physical. Such happened to a devout Maryland priest named Father Richard Scott – who was celebrating Mass in front of about 200 congregants when a stranger entered.

That morning, feast day of Guadalupe, Father Scott, who was trying to make a major decision, had prayed to the Blessed Mother – Queen of Angels – for a sign.

"Blessed Mother," he had said, "I know you are Our Lady of Guadalupe. I'm not worthy, but because of the merits of your Son Jesus and His Divine Mercy, I humbly beseech you to send St. Raphael to give me a sign that what I have heard in my heart is from your Son."

That night Father Scott celebrated a Mass at 7:30 p.m. in honor of the Guadalupe Virgin. He was saying the prayer of the faithful and then watching preparation of the gifts brought to the altar when he suddenly spotted "this young man in his twenties with light brown hair with a big picture, a big painting in a frame, with a luminous face and like an aura around his body.

"He looked different — but completely human, nicely dressed, with corduroy pants, a shirt, a sweater, and like a suede jacket," the priest told me. "He was radiant — the most penetrating eyes! They exuded love, and he had a huge smile — as if he was my best friend – and he walked like he was on a mission to fulfill what God wanted him to do. He strode up the aisle reverently but as if he was in control and nothing would stop him. He just came up, but he didn't do it in a way that was pompous. He didn't float. He walked like a normal person, but quickly with this big painting on his right side and it was like there was a light, a spotlight, on him — like an aura around his body — even though his body was normal, and throughout the whole thing his eyes were in contact with me. He gave reverence to the Eucharist, to me as a priest, genuflected near the tabernacle, and presented this painting. Then he laid it against a lectern on the left-hand side.

"It was a replica of the famous Michelangelo masterpiece, 'The Creation,' in which God is touching the finger of Adam," continued Father Scott. "He went up two steps and laid it against the lectern and said, 'You have to bless it.'

"Even as he said this, his facial expressions never changed. There was complete love and tenderness but he was there on a mission. I couldn't walk up to him. I couldn't *move*."

The congregants were equally shocked. Who was this? No one had ever seen him before. No one saw him again.

"Something kept me from moving," recalled the priest. "I couldn't speak. All I could do was to observe. Afterwards he turned around, genuflected again to the Blessed Sacrament, and then went down the aisle, quickly turned around, looked at me, raised up his arms to Heaven as if he was exuberantly happy, and said with a smile, 'Amen, alleluia!'

"After saying that, he put his arms down and I don't know how the wooden doors opened, but as he was going down the steps, before he got outside I saw him disappear. He went down five or six steps and disappeared. *I saw him disappear.* I did not see the glass doors open, and from the altar I can tell when people leave Mass early. He disappeared just before he got to the glass doors."

Chapter 29

'Illuminated by shafts of light'

A simple prayer: "Angels be with us."

Such helped a woman who was nearly mugged in Queens.

She invoked angels and police later found that she wasn't mugged because the criminal thought he saw two large men on either side of her.

Of course, there was no one there.

"Experience the presence of the angels next to you and allow yourselves to be guided by them," one sage recommended to me.

"Every word of God is tested," says Scripture. "He is a shield to those who take refuge in Him."

Hurricane Katrina?

"I just want to relay a personal story, that happened to a friend and co-worker, an event that happened to him during a hurricane relief effort," wrote Lee Mayeux of Baton Rouge. "A newly formed Knights of Columbus group in Pierre Part, Louisiana (near Morgan City) had taken it upon themselves to contribute to the relief effort in south Louisiana. They started cooking meals for evacuees at different shelters and providing ice in bulk to those in need.

"That week they cooked and transported 3,500 meals and over 13,000 pounds of ice to evacuees at Nicholls State University in Thibodaux. After coming home from a late Friday night feeding, they heard a plea on the radio from State Representative Ben Nevers to help the people of Washington Parish (North of Lake Ponchartrain) because no aid had arrived and the people there were in dire straits. They called each other in the late hours of the night and decided to do something about it.

"There was no time, or food left, to cook so they decided to fire up the ice machines and haul as much as they could. They got to the first ice machine and the loading conveyor had broken, so they shoveled ice. They got to the second ice machine and the bagger had broken, so they shoveled ice. In all three men shoveled 5,000 pounds of ice into an insulated truck and began their journey. It's a good three-hour drive from Pierre Part to Washington Parish.

"They arrived in Washington Parish and met up with the local sheriff.

They were then escorted to town, where overnight several 18-wheelers full of food and water had shown up.

"At this point the men were frustrated and wondering why they had even made the trip. They asked the sheriff if anyone needed the ice. The sheriff said there may be one more place — a shelter a couple miles away that no one has checked on in a couple of days. The three men followed the directions and found the shelter, eventually finding the person in charge.

"They stepped out of the truck and met an older woman wearing a Red Cross uniform who asked if she could help them. The men responded that they had a truck full of ice and wanted to know if they needed any at the shelter. The woman, now beginning to tear up, explained to the men that she and a group had been praying all night for ice to come the next day. And no less than ten minutes earlier had said a prayer to St. Michael asking for a 'truck full of ice.' The men were humbled and thankful to now see that they were being used in part of God's plan. They themselves hadn't eaten all day and after shoveling ice, driving three hours, and experiencing the frustration of roadblock after roadblock, were now full of energy. They helped set up a freezer system for the food which was arriving later that day from the Red Cross and gave all 5,000 pounds of ice to the shelter.

"After all was said and done, the lady in charge asked the three men their names. The men, now smiling, replied 'Michael, Michael, and Michael,' which were indeed their names."

As humans we have no idea how many times our angels have come to our aid, but we can be sure the number is enormous. Usually, in keeping with their humility, their presence is anonymous. God sends them. Do they coordinate coincidence? Shortly after a Baptist music director named Nathan Robinson arrived at a store to buy a new electronic piano and a soundboard – replacing equipment that had been stolen — in walked a young man carrying the church's Yamaha keyboard and hoping to sell the stolen item to the store! Robinson alerted the store's management and they got the equipment back.

Miraculous beings are all around, especially during hardships. When Ronald Reagan was shot, he said there were comforting nurses clad in white hovering around him, giving him crucial comfort even though what fascinated those he related the description to was that the nurses at that hospital did not wear white; they wore *blue*. That same year, Pope John Paul II survived an assassination attempt when the bullet took a path that missed his aorta and major organs – a course that surgeons described as "miraculous" (and which the Pope credited to the Virgin of Fatima, on whose anniversary the shooting occurred).

In the days after September 11, a mysterious man playing a trumpet was spotted in the restricted zone near the World Trade Center. Photographers spotted him on September 18 and tried to snap pictures of him playing his trumpet in the wake of the disaster, said one newspaper, but their shutters jammed mysteriously. One of the witnesses was a well-known photographer who goes by the name of Miklos. As reported by the newspaper, "After hearing a report about the trumpeter on WNYC radio, Miklos said, he went to Ground Zero to photograph him. In the eerie quiet of lower Manhattan, he could hear a trumpet as he approached a police barricade. About 150 yards away, Miklos says, the trumpeter stood 'in this abandoned urban canyon, illuminated by shafts of light caused by the smoke and dust.'" The article went on to say that Miklos raised his telephoto lens, feeling he had "an incredible image" — the photograph of a lifetime — but he couldn't depress the shutter and so never got the shot. The same happened to other photographers. Angels do not want to be visibly documented.

Angelic formations are often seen in clouds. Mainly, they are invisible.

"The times that angels have appeared to me in their full glory it was almost unbearable," noted Dr. Storm, the atheist who had a near-death brush. "The brightness of the light that radiates from them is brighter than the light from a welding torch. Their light doesn't burn the eye, but it is frightening because it is so different from our experience of life. An experience of the supernatural glory and power of an angel is frightening. They don't appear to us in their natural state very often. They most often tone it down for us to keep us comfortable. I don't have the words adequately to describe angels in their natural state. Brighter than lightning, beautiful beyond comparison, powerful, loving, and gentle are words that fail to describe them. The artists' depictions of angels are pitifully inadequate. As an artist I am aware of the impossibility of representing an angel. How do you paint something that is more radiant than substance? How do you paint colors that you have never seen before or since? How do you describe love on a canvas? Why they intervene sometimes and other times don't is between them and God. They told me that they always want to intervene in our lives but God restrains them. God wants us to experience the consequences of our actions. On special rare occasions, God allows the angels to help. When we ask God for spiritual gifts of love, faith, and hope, God always allows the angels to help us. Spiritual gifts are never refused if we are ready to receive them. The angels are working all the time to give us the love of God, faith in God, hope in God. Angels hear our prayers."

They exude love. They rush to help. They respond to prayers of the fervent – that extra special level of faith. "Something caught my eye," said the New York woman who was rescued from would-be muggers by a stranger. "I looked across the street to the other side. A tall young man, with shoulder-length curly blond hair was in the middle of the avenue, heading towards the stop. His face was beautiful. He had a very strong forehead. As he walked, his hair bounced and somehow the light caught his shiny blond curls. As I said, it was night, and it was dark. But, at that distance, from the other side of the street, I could make out the color of his eyes. They were a shining, sparkling blue — ice-blue, piercing eyes. He was very strong looking; determination was written all over his face. He had a serious look on his face, not angry just serious like when someone is on a mission. My heart jumped with joy and relief. I was not alone anymore. He came and stood right next to me. He didn't say anything, he didn't look my way. He was very tall, white complexion. It's been about ten years since that happened and in my mind I can still see him crystal clear as if it was yesterday. What I remember most of all are the sparkling, piercing blue eyes. They were like two stars in the night. And his beautiful, curly blond hair bouncing as he walked, framing his strong forehead. Handsome, but he did not inspire human attraction, rather, respect and awe because you could feel his strength, not physical but a strength that I cannot describe."

Nothing evil can touch them. They also bring us the lesson of joy. *Angels are often described as joyful* and perhaps it is joy that is their weapon.

Joy cuts a huge swath through even a landslide of negativity.

I know this from personal experience. One time out of the blue a company that was funding a major project of mine suddenly killed the project. It was no minor thing. In fact, most men who have to support their families would have found it devastating. At many times in my life, I would have also reacted that way. It would have been a tragedy! I had been working on this project for a year – had traveled around America and from Europe to Japan researching material for it – and it was to provide enough money for our family to live on for at least three years. In fact, it was the most money I had ever been offered. When it fell through I took the joyful approach, all but totally ignored the "evil report," and surrendered. Those who knew about it were confused by my response – it seemed like a cruel injustice had been committed against us – but almost immediately a far greater project came my way.

I can't tell you how great it was to rise above that "cloud of darkness"!

There are no clouds when we take flight with the God of miracles.

Smile at those who detest you, send joy to those who persecute you, and your enemies will be made into your footstools. As Scripture advises, "let those who love Him be like the rising of the sun in its might" (*Judges* 5:31).

When compassion is around us and when it is projected to others, it disarms even those who are hostile. The key is to approach every person with a smile. Mother Teresa said that "holy living consists of doing God's work with a smile." She also said that the smile on a child was God's love. Let us imitate the angels, who are usually described with a smile and whose love radiates a sense of strength.

A smile is a powerful spiritual tool, announces that we are of a benevolent disposition (when there is true emotion behind it), and allows us to stop focusing so much on ourselves. It's only when we have pride that we become sullen and engulfed in depression, which comes from self-absorption.

If we have abandoned ourselves, and eliminated the "self" (with joy), we're not concerned about being "insulted."

An insult can only take hold if there is pride. It is also the fuel of discord. We have insecurities when we have pride, which cause us to "clamp up." We frown. We withdraw. Those with ebullient, outgoing personalities break down the pretensions of those who otherwise would be insulting. It keeps away the enemy because joy springs from love, love is God, Who is also Light, and light dispels darkness.

Chapter 30

God wants you to enhance the dignity of others

Being nice is important in spiritual development, glorifies the Lord, and unlocks the door to what God has in store for us.

It means to be considerate. It means to see through the eyes of those we encounter.

It means to place others ahead of ourselves.

And it means mundane things like being punctual. To be kind is to be considerate, helpful, and make every effort to lift another person's day – to affect other lives for the better.

We could change the world if this happened with just a small percentage of us. There is the "chain reaction" reaction mentioned by Barbara, who during her near-death experience saw the "circle of light" around the world. That "chain" operates in both the natural and the supernatural. On the invisible level, niceness generates a light that revolves around our existence, swathing us with a band of goodness. That light reflects on our physical being and makes us attractive. Didn't you ever notice how beautiful a holy person looks even if he or she is not actually physically "attractive"? We can all do that. Anytime goodness is projected, it has an actual force. Goodness creates light around us, and we can tap into that, while negativity adds to darkness and causes us to tap into the negative. Goodness erases the "circle of dark," and it also operates on a practical level. Think of it: when you let someone in front of you, that person is far more prone to take similar action with someone else. There is an atmosphere of niceness. We feel better, and in the realm of the supernatural, we actually cause a light to shine from God – whereas selfishness brings down a cloud. In your day-to-day life, notice how when you act the wrong way toward a person or situation, it negatively charges the atmosphere.

How do we tell what is right and wrong in our relationships?

In life it is always crucial to consider the dignity of other people and to gauge every action we take or word we speak (or even thought we think) on how it could *affect* that dignity. This is also a good way of judging whether something is a sin, and is true whether it is in a casual circumstance or the intimacy of a sexual relationship: an affront to dignity is a transgression. It doesn't matter whether it's an insult, a business transaction, a case of overcharging others, gossip, using another for sexual purposes, or cheating on a spouse. Anything that lessens another and puts you "above" that person, as superior, demonstrates pride and subtracts from the grace God wants to shed upon us. Treating others as we would want to be treated, the "golden rule," has the opposite effect. When we make an effort that always has the other person in mind, God grants us fulfillment. We gain His stock of miracles.

That consideration is most easily reached by bringing ourselves into the practice of love, which automatically upholds the dignity of others.

In wondering if you should do something, you should always ask how it will make the other person feel about himself. Am I feeding goodness and love into his soul? How will whatever I plan to do affect my own perception of that person?

When we are mean to someone, we lower that person's image. We're treating the other person as inferior. Being short with someone who doesn't deserve it is an insult, and while the other person may rise above that insult, it lowers you spiritually. Even thinking negatively about a person can affect that person's self-image. We are spiritual beings, and we often receive information from the thoughts, words, body language, and actions of others. If I am always late for an appointment with you, what does that tell me about the worth I associate with the meeting?

On the other hand, kindness resonates as a "love demonstration." God doesn't care whether you were the world-record holder for the shot-put, or a world-class lawyer, or a brilliant pianist. What He wants to know is how you *conducted* yourself as a lawyer or musician or world-record holder for the shot-put. How have you handled yourself in your station of life? When Christ evaluates your life, He will show you how many of the things you considered great achievements were not so great while He fills you with joy each time He shows you the fruit of your kindness, however "small" the act seems.

When we lack kindness, there is a void. There is a vacancy we feel around ourselves or others.

Chapter 31

Let your abilities blossom

Kindness is a spark that reflects God's Light while hate engulfs us in an actual darkness. When we're kind, joy begins to creep into our being, and then to pervade it. Our bodies and emotions are both healthier. Our cells react to kindness and are often healed of sickness. Kindness is wishing another well, and so it is a blessing. We receive blessings in return. As one writer noted, kindness drives gloom and darkness from our souls and replaces it with hope. It glorifies, it ennobles, it purifies. It beautifies us. *We actually look better.* To ennoble is to increase dignity. It builds up. It summons grace where discouragement resists those gifts that God has in store for us.

"Kindness adds sweetness to everything," notes an author named Lawrence G. Lovasik. "It makes life's capabilities blossom and fills them with fragrance."

Those who are spiritually gifted are often accompanied by a mysterious odor of sanctity, an aroma that resembles a combination of lilies and roses.

Kindness opens a portal to the hereafter and through that portal comes surprise.

Angels watch our every move and celebrate when we perform an act of goodness. When we need them, they speed on the highway that our love has paved.

Kindness is potent because it is active love.

One kind word, one kind smile, one gesture, is often enough to serve as a catalyst.

We don't see it, but the world around us changes.

The legend goes of a stranger who sought shelter for the night and was tossed out when he uttered God's Name in vain. In the morning, an angel appeared to the innkeeper, exclaiming, "I sent a stranger to you for shelter. Where is he?" When the innkeeper explained what happened, the angel replied: "For forty years God has been patient with that man. For one single night could you not bear with him?"

Patience and forbearance are the stuff of angels and the stuff of miracles. Think of all the times your guardian has stood by you despite *your* conduct.

The Book of Proverbs tells us that "a patient man is better than a warrior, and he who rules his temper, than he who takes a city."

This forbearance leads to the grace of knowing ourselves more intimately, and brings about a housecleaning.

It is an exercise in discipline, and discipline strengthens the Spirit. With discipline you can control your emotions and reorient your thoughts. Discipline is like the side of a river. Without its banks, a river becomes a swamp. Control keeps matters in check. I mentioned darkness. Are there really demons? There are demons and they attach to negativity. They darken our moods. They instill thoughts. They send us discouragement. They scorn. They cause us to be desperate. They certainly inhibit our faith. They haunt our dreams. They make others say or do things that harass us. Some people give them names. There is a "spirit of lust," which entices us to sins of the flesh. There is a "spirit of anger," which can be anything from temper to murder. There are spirits of "infirmity," which cause illness. If you study the case histories of famous crimes, you'll often find the footprints of evil and even "voices" that told the criminal to do what he did. Apparently without realizing it, John Lennon had been tapping into darkness. He had held séances in his apartment, the Dakota, which also had been the setting for an occult movie, *Rosemary's Baby,* which starred Mia Farrow. His band had written one song, *Helter Skelter,* that "influenced' Charles Manson, who killed Sharon Tate, wife of the movie's director. The assassin later described the way voices had urged him to kill the famous singer, and in a final irony, the last person the killer saw before he shot Lennon was Farrow walking her dog.

In our own lives the influence normally is subtle and works in the subconscious. These are creatures of the "dark" and their presence can be hard to detect. They are often the cause of what seem like run-of-the mill problems: anxiety, obsession, oppression, and depression (note the hi*ss*). In fact, many maladies that we categorize as psychological are actually spiritual, which is why psychology has a low success rate with many emotional disturbances: if we look at the most radical "psychological" illnesses (such as multiple-personality), we can see the infiltration of alien ideas, notions, and personalities, which is another way of saying "spirits."

Anything that is cold, vacant, and leaves us with a feeling of aridity immediately should be suspicious. Another hallmark is confusion. Spirits come and go. They can be indigenous to a home, a neighborhood, a city, a region. *Ephesians* tells us that "our battle is not against human forces but against the principalities and powers, the rulers of this world of darkness, the evil spirits in regions above" (6:12) and in *Daniel* we see how a powerful demon held sway over the entire region of Persia.

More commonly they're of lesser power but can attach to our spirits. They cause a cloud to form, and they can come down the generations, causing problems like alcoholism, suicide, and divorce, which occur in some families with a frequency that otherwise defies explanation.

Often the first indication of evil is anxiety. Fear is a great device of Satan, who likes to make himself look bigger than he is. Fear can manifest as angst, apprehensiveness, cowardice, doubt, dread, faintheartedness, phobias, suspicions, timidity, or simple worry. We fear disgrace, incompetence, condemnation, disapproval, failure, and lost of respect – most of which are rooted in pride. When you feel fear come, settle into prayer and specifically command the "spirit of fear" away (and then ask the Lord to cast away any other spirit that may be plaguing you; He will guide you on what you need to do, which may involve fasting).

Our entire time on earth is spent dueling with these forces and most of the time we don't even know what we're battling. The vast majority of people spend their lives oblivious to the cause of their most intransigent problems.

How does this occur? Demons come through sin, unforgiveness, or spiritual neglect, which is another way of saying sloth and is one of the seven "deadly" sins. They are "deadly" because they can manifest as illness (or fatal habits).

Laziness tends toward evil. So does unbelief. When we doubt God or otherwise commit sin, we are drawn toward the fog that Storm encountered. We also hinder the miraculous power that God wants to send. When you feel blocked in your life, head into prayer and ask what it is that has brought the blockage. Spirits come when we hate or lust. They come through drugs, smoking, and overuse of alcohol. They come very powerfully through infidelity. When we have an illicit relationship, we are "one" with that person and share his or her spirits. Other spirits come from the shows we watch and the literature we read.

Beware especially of the occult. By this I mean astrology, mind-reading, Ouija boards, séances, mediums, psychics, clairvoyance, Santeria, "evil-eye" horns, witchcraft, pagan worship, nature gods, goddesses, wizards, or the New Age. It is well known that tragic "coincidences" have followed movies such as *The Exorcist* based on occult themes. (In a remake of the film, the director quit in the middle of it and shortly after suffered a stroke, a key actor unexpectedly dropped out, the new director was fired, his replacement was struck by a car, and there were what the press reported as "spooky premonitions.")

The earth is a dynamic place and there is a constant interplay between good and evil. Christ was not using metaphors when He spoke of demons. The mute. The paralytic. The "demented." Spirits can cause infirmities. They can at least aggravate illness. They attach themselves to us when they find a chink in our armor. If we are inclined to something evil, even in thought, and if we allow such thoughts to linger, they attach to us.

Sin blocks the Holy Spirit and the reason is that at the root of nearly every sin is a lack of kindness. Think about lust: this is the sexual use of another without love. Think of theft: when we steal from someone, we are demonstrating anything but kindness. Think about dishonoring our parents, and using the Name of God in vain, and all the other violations of commandments: they are rooted in a lack of love, and since God is love and love is the energy behind miracles, we shut ourselves off.

The same is true of extremes. A cardinal rule is that the devil is a man of extremes, and whenever we're out of balance, there is a loophole that he's only too happy to exploit. We can eat too little, allowing him to manifest in anorexia, or too *much* (giving him an entrance through the sin of gluttony). We can be lazy or, at the other extreme — if we are diligent — the devil may tempt us to overdo it as a workaholic.

Anything that goes to the far end of a spectrum, anything with *"too"* or *"overly"* in front of it, and anything that hinders other aspects of life, tends toward darkness.

Often, we open ourselves to evil in ways that don't seem like sin. Here we get into the realm of "imperfections" – and they too stunt the miraculous life.

All of us are here on earth to correct such imperfections, and when we don't, when we don't come into balance, there is the intrusion of darkness.

Have we not all found ourselves in runs of misfortune? Have we not all seen situations that seem to go in vicious cycles?

This can happen in many ways, and it behooves us to purge them, for as I said, when there is blockage our lives are not prone to intervention. We hear the term "wrestling with demons," and so it is. Throughout our lives, there are two voices, that of our angels (encouraging us and suggesting good) and the voice of darkness that draws us toward discouragement. Is there not a constant internal dialogue?

We must resolve to heed only the angels, which means the Holy Spirit. Looking back, we will note that many unfortunate circumstances in our lives, and certainly our unfortunate habits, are because we have lacked discipline. So important is self-control that Jesus demonstrated it for us by fasting for forty days – at which time he was able to fend off the devil.

When we have control over the flesh, the Holy Spirit, the spirit of discipline, is with us. When we don't have discipline, we fall into every kind of problem. Thoughts of lust can become an addiction to pornography, or to acts of fornication and adultery, which strip us of a connection to God. Thoughts of jealousy can become thoughts of hatred and selfishness can grow into greed. Thoughts of overindulgence can tend toward obesity, drugs, or alcoholism. Thoughts of skepticism can turn into a lack of faith (and even atheism, the most dangerous of all sins).

Our "flesh," our worldly inclinations, are at constant war with our spiritual side, which is why those who are skeptical about the power of the Holy Spirit tend to be those whose focus is on the material. It's a lifelong battle. The Lord sets us here to develop mastery over sinful inclinations. This is because such spiritual mastery develops us. Each time we conquer a lustful thought, each time we grow in discipline, our spirits flourish and we find greater closeness to Him. Look at the incredible self-discipline of Jesus: not only His fasting, but the way He controlled His emotions to the point of forgiving those responsible for His Crucifixion at the height of His pain.

The goal is to get to the point where we can immediately extinguish each thought that may inhibit the growth of our spirits. During life, we make mistakes, and that's okay — as long as we don't repeat them. True contrition makes sure of that and expands the spirit. It has an effect that cleanses. And God, Who is pure, melds with us in proportion to our purity. Cleanliness is next to godliness as long as it doesn't become obsessive and purity necessitates discipline.

The vast majority of sins germinate progressively in our thoughts. While the first thing that comes into mind is not a sin, keeping an evil thought and dwelling on it is. Thoughts spread like wildfire. Once we let such a thought repeat, it is "seeded." From there, it takes root (cultivated by Satan).

The key is to step back and pray until such a thought has been erased. Once we clear our thoughts, we have an opportunity to maintain a pure conscience. It is important that we do so. Besides exposing us to evil, negative thoughts infringe on the simplest miracle in daily life, which is happiness. We may not notice it, but a good day often takes a turn toward a bad one with *a single bad thought,* and so it's at that very moment that we have to sweep away the seed.

If someone has slighted you, there is an opportunity to spiritually advance by replacing ill thoughts with kindness. Do not "drink of the poison." Do not fall for the temptation that the devil offers you. Remember that nun in the case of Dr. Storm. Instead of taking insult at what he had said, she kept her "stream" pure and the result was a miracle.

Chapter 32

Don't drink of the poison

All through our lives, we too encounter attempts at poisoning us, and all it takes is a drop to contaminate. Think of the times that a little insult – a beep of the horn, a rude voice on the other end of the line – has ruined your day.

Now take that memory a step further. Think it over and you will realize that the insult affected your entire day only because you let it. You reacted to it, which means you drank of its poison. You accepted a shipment of rattlesnakes.

This is a very important spiritual lesson: insult does not affect us unless we allow it to. Mainly, it happens through unforgiveness. When we don't forgive always and instantly, we set negative forces in motion.

Everyone gets hurt in life. We face disappointments, losses, and stress. If this has provoked ill thoughts, the response should be Confession. When we withhold forgiveness to "get even," we are rendering evil for evil.

Initial sting? Yes. Insult will often sting no matter how we react. But if we refuse to dwell on it and immediately forgive, going beyond, it loses its venom.

We "drink of the poison" when we react to it. The wrong reaction will cause the actions or words of others to attach themselves. We all have experienced the difficulty of removing a weed once it takes root. We yank and it won't come out. The roots are a foot deep and got there in a hurry. It's incredible how quickly weeds can root! The same is true of evil: When we allow it into our lives, even for a moment, it takes root very quickly and becomes all but impossible to pull out. A good day turns bad and gets worse. Pretty soon, we're sliding down a mountain (and toward a ledge). On the other hand, when we exercise mercy, forgive immediately, and see beyond the insult, weeds have nowhere to drill their roots.

Love casts away evil.

So does mercy.

The first thing we should think of when people aggravate us is why they may have aggravated us – whether through unthinking, something in their own pasts, or something that they are going through.

In many cases, they don't mean anything by it.

This realization helps us see beyond the insult and remain with the Miracle Worker. I'm not saying that we should never admonish. Often, we're called to correct those who are errant. But the important point – and the way to connect with God – is to make sure we do not judge or harbor a grudge.

When Scripture tells us to judge the sin but not the sinner, this is because we can't possibly know why a certain person is the way he is. True, it can be a simple result of that person's evil; it could stem from a person's self-centeredness. This is the root of many negative personality traits. But it could also be the way the insulting persons was "made" — which is to say that the reason for bad behavior may be a "cross" that has been inherited. The person who offends may be fighting demons we can't see.

Seeing beyond evil takes love and love develops through prayer, lessening fear. We can train ourselves to love. We can practice. If we're having a difficult time loving someone, we should imagine that person as an infant.

Doesn't that make it easier? Isn't it hard to hate a youngster? And isn't that how God sees us? Or simply view life as a cause for Christ. It is not about you. It is about Him. Watch that take the heat off.

There are other "tricks of the trade," and they're important because without a loving spirit we are simply not open to what God wants to send. If it is a close relative you're having trouble with, imagine how you would feel if that person were to die today. Would you feel remorse at disliking that person? Would you regret the way you left things? Is the dispute worth parting on a bitter note?

If you're still having trouble, ask yourself: Have I really taken the time in prayer to imagine every reason why that person is the way he is or why he may have done or said what he did?

This helps to empathize with a hostile person and when we don't, we leave the way open to a spiritual blockage, which may be another way of saying a "curse."

Contention with another makes us vulnerable to that person's ill feelings. There is a hole in our bubble.

Spiritual rule: unless absolutely necessary, do not engage with antagonists. When provoked, step back and say to yourself (as many times as you need), "I don't have to get into a fight over that." It's that simple. When we step back, we give God room to function.

It's when we engage with someone who is attacking or bothering us or even talk about that the sting, the nettle, the venom, remains.

Talking about evil can give it power; a curse is born.

When we focus on an itch, or play around with a cut, it gets worse and there can be an infection. We all know that a small infection (in an innocuous place like your finger) can become systemic, affecting the entire body.

So too does infection take root in the dimension of spirits. The more we focus on it, the more the evil presents itself. That puts us under a cloud. It blocks grace. When people are mad, they are often wishing negative things upon us and those negative desires will land *if we give them the opportunity to*. When we ignore insult, it closes the door to infiltration.

One of the greatest tests of life thus is to do this, to turn the other cheek. If we love whoever insults us and return good for evil, harboring no ill will, the curse will not "alight," to use the expression from *Proverbs*. This is why Christ told us to turn the other cheek. When we release resentment, we're joining forces with the way He forgave on the Cross. As we endure an irritation patiently, the wound heals and the way to the miraculous opens. Love in all circumstances. Forgiveness is an extra step toward love.

One woman wrote to me about a husband who desperately needed a kidney transplant. A crisis this was, with no exit. There was only one person who matched his blood type — a sister who was estranged.

They had a back and forth with her, and finally, to the horror of all, the sister announced that she had reached a decision and didn't want to donate the organ.

She wouldn't do it. And it was galling. It was devastating. Now, the woman's husband had only weeks to live.

But remarkably, instead of harboring bitterness, this man's wife had stepped back, settled down to prayer, and through prayer came to her own remarkable decision. She would forgive the sister. No matter what, there would be love. Evil would not be returned for evil. She prepared a letter of forgiveness.

But at the last minute, before the letter reached her, the sister changed her mind and offered her kidney against all expectation.

Indeed, God is the God of the last second! It's a mystery why we must suffer such things, but from it is a path toward perfection. Difficulty punctures a hole in our pride, drains it away, and affords us the opportunity to love. Forgiveness is a manifestation of love that is projected outwardly.

Letting one's thoughts hover over an aggravation is completely counterproductive and can be stopped only through discipline. That means controlling what you think. In your head is that constant inner dialogue and you have to make sure that it's devoid of anger. At the first negative thought, step back and halt the thought. Dismiss it. Command it away. Do this every time it comes. Soon, doing so will be easy.

There is nothing that should gall you because there is absolutely nothing anyone has ever done that goes unseen by God and will not be addressed by Him in due course here or in the hereafter.

It is a spiritual truth that "what goes around comes around." In some way, we get what we have meted out — often here on earth and often when we least expect it. The more problems we cause, the more problems we subsequently experience, while the more we love, the more we forgive, especially when it's hard to forgive, and especially when we were right, the more love is subsequently returned to us (often when we most need it).

Conversely, when we criticize others, we often "jinx" ourselves to the same failing. By that I mean that we bring the same failing into our own lives – the same fault for which we have criticized someone now comes upon *us* — and we are tested. When we hover on the failure of someone else, a situation will arise that tests *our* ability to avoid the same kind of mistake in our own lives. We may criticize another person for being cheap and then find ourselves in a situation that dearly tests our willingness to give.

I remember the account of a professional thief. His entire livelihood was stealing from others. He was a house burglar. If he couldn't con someone out of money (as a home-repair man), he came back when they weren't around. Later, he was arrested in a sensational gangland killing and turned into a state witness against his fellow criminals. In retribution, those former "friends" then set about stripping his home of every single thing he ever owned, even the most trivial possession. He became the biggest victim of burglary that anyone knew. The boomerang had returned.

The opposite happens when we give. The more we give – and forgive — the more we receive.

"God wants to set you free," says one healing priest. "He wants to heal you – spirit, soul, and body. However, we can never be completely freed and healed until we forgive: forgiveness is the foundation for all healing. Many times unforgiveness is also accompanied by hate, resentment, revenge, anger, and bitterness. If we allow these negative emotions to remain in our spirits, we perhaps end up with a physical problem such as arthritis, high blood pressure, stomach problems, colitis, or heart problems. If you have one or all of these diseases, we are not saying that unforgiveness is the root cause, but we are saying that many times these emotions do cause physical problems."

The priest cites the case of a woman who would not forgive her husband's girlfriend. The wife was suffering from arthritis that had crippled her. The pain was excruciating. A nun prayed with her and helped her see the necessity for forgiveness. The nun had an advanced degree in counseling and said it was the most astonishing case she had ever witnessed. The woman prayed and forgave the other woman and immediately her pain left. She was able to get out of bed and serve refreshments.

Ignore the insult. Curse not others. Forgive beyond tolerance. *Love especially when it is most difficult!* "Wrath and anger are hateful things, yet the sinner hugs them tight," says the Book of Sirach (27:30-28:7). "The vengeful will suffer the Lord's vengeance, for He remembers their sins in detail. Forgive your neighbor's injustice; then when you pray, your own sins will be forgiven. Could anyone nourish anger against another and expect healing from the Lord?"

"Early in my ministry the Lord taught me that lack of forgiveness can hinder us from being healed and having our prayers answered," notes Dr. Bob Rice. "A woman in my church named Betty had very poor eyesight. At one of our Sunday night services, Betty came to me for prayers for her eyes. As I began to pray for her, the Lord stopped me from praying. The Lord told me that Betty lacked forgiveness in her heart toward her sister-in-law and that He would not heal her eyes until she went to her sister-in-law. She was to forgive her sister-in-law and ask for forgiveness for all the problems they had between them for so many years."

The woman knew what he was talking about, did as she was told, says Rice, and was instantly healed.

It says in Scripture that God will forgive if you forgive, and if you don't, you still bear a great hindrance. Where love is lacking so is healing. We need to go through our lives and with sincere, open hearts forgive every person who in any way may have offended us (and at any point since birth, or even conception). Parents. Siblings. Cousins. Aunts. Friends. Employers. Classmates. Even passersby. "Lord Jesus Christ, I wish to come to You today to forgive *everyone* in my life, and I know You will give me the strength I need to forgive them," is one prayer you can say and as you delve into it, you'll be astonished at who and what comes to mind. *All of us have been offended in ways we nearly have forgotten and as a result have deeply hid-*

den pockets of "unforgiveness."

This stifles us. It is more inhibiting than you realize. As the Holy Spirit brings out pockets of unforgiveness, forgive everyone in every situation you can think of. Step back, spend time releasing all negative emotions, and replace them with positive feelings. Was there a relative who subjected you to abuse? Or someone who slandered you? Who falsely accused you? Who betrayed you as a friend? Was there a boyfriend or girlfriend who rejected you? Send forgiveness to that person — no matter how hard it seems (and no matter how unworthy the person). Was there a teacher who caused you have to lower self-esteem? A coach? A neighbor?

When we can't stomach a person, or when we have taken an insult to heart, it can end up affecting the heart or stomach! "Lord, I forgive my brothers and sisters for rejecting me, hating me, resenting me, competing for my parents' love…"

When the forgiveness of others, especially family members, is complete (or nearly complete, since we constantly have to forgive), we also have to forgive ourselves. You'd be surprised how inhibited you are because you still hold something against yourself! It stands in the way of a full relationship with Jesus.

The biggest stumbling block is often the feeling that we are not good enough – that we don't deserve to be healed – and we need to step back and release that. We have to let go of sins we have already confessed or this too will block us.

Satan is the great accuser and causes you to bring negative aspects into your life as sort of self-punishment, blocking graces that God has in store when really it is up to God to judge.

Chapter 33

The real root of all evil

Ask the Lord to purify you of what you need to purify, and beyond all else, make certain that you have forgiven the Lord! As astonishing as it seems, there are many people who are angry with God. Talk about a block! How can God help us when we have a resistance to Him?

Anger toward God is the single greatest obstacle to grace. Never let such an emotion take hold.

I once knew a man whose wife was dying of cancer. He was a good man, but it was too tough on him, and I heard him say he was angry at God. He became very embittered. That made me quake because I felt that he was lowering his protection. And within a couple years, he too died prematurely. Anger had hardened his heart to the point of a coronary attack, and had opened a susceptibility to the enemy.

Nothing blocks the miraculous like resentment of God, whether that resentment is spoken or unspoken. Let us all pray not to be tested. God is never to blame. What we have to do is faithfully place it into His Hands and wait, patiently, even over minor issues. For years, I was "aggravated" because I swim everyday and at one health club it was getting hard. Most of the folks were doing aerobic-type exercises, walking in the water, or simply using the pool as a social club, standing there and chatting while I was trying to do laps. There was a very large fellow who was always walking in front of swimmers; and he was constantly there — spending hours in the pool and collecting a group around him. When he wasn't doing that, he was walking the width of the pool, effectively shutting it off.

On countless occasions I had to fight off agitation. There was the temptation to confront him, or to have a chat with the lifeguards. Every time he blocked me off, I had to struggle not to be angry. I resolved to let God handle it, and to love that man (who wasn't the friendliest in the world) each time he cut off my lane or otherwise aggravated me.

That worked the miracle.

Suddenly, one day, right after I had conquered my negative feelings, a rope of buoys went up across the entrance to the deep end. It turned out that the big guy couldn't swim and the lifeguards realized that when nonswimmers were in the pool, they were obligated to rope off the deep end. When the rope was up, those who walked around blocking the lanes could no longer wander into the deep-end and I could now go into that end of the pool and swim with no interference.

I began to look forward to seeing the big guy, because the only trouble I now had was when he *wasn't* there (because, then, the buoys weren't in place). They could no longer cut me off!

God had taken a situation that seemed impossible to resolve (without conflict), turning it into a situation I could not have engineered on my own.

In response to my patience, He had turned a "curse" into a blessing.

In no circumstance will you *not* be vindicated if you trust in the Lord.

It may not be as quickly as you like, but it will happen if you simply let go of it.

In most circumstances, when someone offends you, you have to pray for that person and victory will come. I have seen many times when someone who started as a bitter enemy ended up as a friend because I ignored a slight. In some way, whoever hurts you will be brought to atone for that hurt. Let God decide how.

Does that mean we never complain? There are times that we have to go through proper channels and make a situation known to the authorities, or to the offending person himself. At times we're called to admonish. But we have to do it with love. We are never to be propelled by the negative. God places situations and people in our lives in order to develop our ability to love, and if we have love, good things occur. When we let Him, God turns us from victims into victors. If you love in all situations, you can find His wonders even in what seems galling.

If there is a temptation to lash out, look upon it as an opportunity to love in difficult circumstances. The more difficult the hurdle, the greater the merit. It is never productive to place your heart in a marinade of bitterness. "A middle-aged woman in a wheelchair had been very angry with God ever since her only two pregnancies had miscarried," a British psychiatrist once reported. "In a church Eucharistic service, she apologized for her anger and prayed for the two children. Suddenly, a hot glow penetrated her whole being, she rose to her feet, and then walked all the way home."

She might have remained a cripple if she had kept hold of her pride, which had cemented her spirit. Pride is the cement of discontent. It is hoarding love.

If you are oppressed or can't find peace, or your prayers are not answered, yes, search for God's Will, but also look for pride. We must work to rectify any such manifestations of it, for *pride above all blocks miracles.* I have mentioned it often because it is the greatest source of spiritual stress and as the thesaurus tells us, pride is self-admiration, self-glorification, self-love, self-sufficiency (in the sense of relying on ourselves instead of God), and vainglory. Pride is jealousy. It is envy. It is a sense (often hidden) of superiority. When there is over-ambition, when there is competition, when there is a constant yearning for more, when you are too easily insulted, it is pride again, and it sends us into a tailspin of anxiety.

Pride blocks happiness and to root it out takes the Holy Spirit.

Upon request, He will search out pride so cleverly rooted that you may never find it.

Many times a major spiritual issue is ingrained to the point where it reveals itself only when we specifically *ask* that it be revealed – at which time it will come to the surface in some fashion. Often God shows us our shortcomings through mysterious sequences of events. *"What is blocking me, Lord? Why am I lacking the miraculous?,"* we do well to ask.

However the answer arrives, and however long it takes, He never fails to answer.

Nothing covers itself up like pride, nothing is trickier to root out, and nothing is more serpentine. Pride is at the root of many sins and is what got Lucifer thrown out of Heaven. Think of the snake wrapped around that tree. Pride coils. Pride camouflages. We think of the obvious ways. It is operative through arrogance, which is what we often think of as pride, or more subtly as impatience (we're too important to wait). It is operative when in any way we feel above others or we give ourselves too much credit. It is greed (*we* deserve the most). It is the feeling of *me first*. It can take the form of anger (when our pride is affronted) or of rejecting others. Many people even have pride in their "spirituality"or are proud that they "don't" have pride.

That's what I mean by trickery, and only the Holy Spirit can discern the subtler manifestations. When we're too self-satisfied, when we think we and we alone have our acts together, when we believe in our exceptional goodness, this should send up a red flag.

Often, pride takes the form of materialism. We are placing earthly riches as our focus, and striving to win the game of life (to end up with the most "toys") means we see ourselves as above our neighbors.

We strive and compete and clench our teeth. At times, we succeed. There are victories.

But those victories are usually fleeting. There will be the devil, the "prince of pride," to pay. *Pride leads to nothing that lasts.* A spiritual law. Instead, it invites in the devil and allows him a piece of our "turf" that is proportionate to our pride.

When evil is around, look for a way you have been proud, for Satan gains entry through the hole it creates in our souls and all joy leaves with his presence. Pride puts us in danger. It strips us of true life. It equals evil, which as I said is the word "live" placed backwards.

Often we see wealthy people and wonder why they have been so greatly "rewarded" for ventures that are purely selfish. On the surface it is almost miraculous. They have a power that we don't. They can send their kids to the Ivy League. They can afford to travel whenever they feel the urge. Cars are toys to them. They seem to have it all. They don't worry about paying the electric bill. It seems like a charmed life.

But most often wealth is a burden, even a curse. When used for selfish purposes it puts us out of touch with the Plan of God, and the life of someone who is out of God's plan is a life of "wonders" that are superficial. All of what we have and are belongs to God, and in some way must be made to serve Him. How we handle our money affects how much God will bless us. "If you have not been trustworthy in handling worldly wealth," says Scripture, "who will trust you with true riches?"

Forget about trying to be a cross between holy and worldly.

Money can be a gift, and like any gift, it is meant for God's glory. When used for that purpose, it's fine. We are meant to do something with money and other gifts we receive. They are meant to help both God and those around us. To live is to give. Note the word "charmed": we don't want to be anointed by the wrong source. To take is of the snake. The Bible says that "you cannot serve both God and mammon."

When we're rich and use that gift only for our *selves*, we are left with only the "wonders" that money can buy, which turn into baggage. God gives us what we need while the devil gives us luxury, which separates us from the truly miraculous. When the billionaire dies, God will be unimpressed with the fact that he was a billionaire unless he had used the money for the good of mankind and the rich man will be astonished at how what he had possessed was not of his own doing (as pride had told him) but in some cases (when it wasn't a reward from the dark side) had been given to him

– entrusted — for a mission he was supposed to perform for the Lord. *Make sure you search for your mission.* When God reviews your life and asks what you have done, He won't be very impressed if you say, "Well, I took the money and bought myself a mansion. I also bought myself a Bentley. I bought the largest yacht and parked it in front of another mansion that was my summer home."

Can you imagine how God will respond to that, and how the billionaire will feel when the Lord explains that the money had been earmarked for *God's* purposes?

There is the expression that money is the root of all evil, but a better translation is probably that "money is the root of all kinds" of evil. The real root of *all* evil is lack of love, *and when we lack love it is often because of our pride.* Pride explains many evils that money cannot (like using another for lustful purposes) and even sits at the root of the love for money. It causes everything from family arguments to war. In fact the manifestations of pride are astounding. It can take the form of anger, selfishness, hypersensitivity, feuding, fear, and a short temper. When we're angry we should ask ourselves *why* we are angry; when we're impatient, we should ask ourselves *why* we are impatient; when we're fearful, we should ask ourselves *why* we are fearful; when we are hateful, we should ask ourselves *why* we are hateful; when we're depressed, we should investigate what is depressing or confusing us – what is causing the anxiety.

Often the answer is "pride." How is this so? We may be angry because someone has insulted us, and that goes to pride because the insult has infringed on our high opinion of ourselves. We may be impatient because we feel that our time is more valuable than another's. We may be fearful because something threatens our standing, and we may be hateful because others have more than we do and we feel we deserve more than *they* do (this is jealousy). We may be anxious because something is threatening our reputations.

Without the right motives, anything we have that makes us proud becomes a danger to the soul and while there may be cash in the bank or a Hummer in the driveway, or a fur to wear, the gratifications eventually will evaporate.

In the void will come an obsession. Many homeless people are happier than multi-millionaires because they don't have that kind of burden. Mother Teresa once called the U.S. the "poorest" nation on earth specifically because of its materialism. Are there good rich people? Of course. There are *holy* rich people. I've met them. But holiness is very difficult when there is money because possessions blind us. They block miracles as they place our focus on the physical and cause us to try turning earth into Heaven.

Sudden windfalls such as winning the lottery or coming into an inheritance does deliver a jolt of happiness, but it's usually fleeting. Studies of multimillion-dollar lottery winners have shown that negatives prevailed for many, with higher rates of alcoholism, divorce, loss of friends, and isolation. A surprising number of "winners" were broke within a decade of their windfall.

A University of Illinois psychologist named Ed Dierner found no difference when he compared the overall well-being of millionaires and billionaires on the Forbes 400 list of the richest Americans with Maasai herdsmen in East Africa (who live in mud huts and wear pieces of tire for shoes). In parts of the Caribbean people are so poor that they resort to mixing dirt with saltwater for food and yet exhibit great gratitude to God for what little they have — a gratitude that brings them the miracle of happiness.

Of course, that's an extreme. Perhaps the best guide is in Scripture: "Two things I ask of you, deny them not to me before I die: put falsehood and lying far from me, give me neither poverty nor riches; provide me only with the food I need" (*Proverbs* 30:7-8).

You get the point: you don't need baggage. And you certainly don't need pride. Self-esteem is one thing; haughtiness is another. There are times that you probably get angry or impatient because of the pride in others. A person who thinks quite a lot of himself may take his time at the automatic teller, letting you wait. This may get your goat because it is hooking into your own remnants of pridefulness. When evil connects with us, it is doing so because it has found a common path. Without pride, a whole new world opens up to us, a world that's focused on God and releases His love – which is the Force of all that is wondrous and the root of all good and every prayer that is answered.

Chapter 34

Don't give the devil a foothold

Any tarnish on our spirits inhibits the flow of grace. It is important to remember that we are called to leave our *mark* in this world, not a blemish.

It is equally important to recognize that the first thing we taint is the spirit.

If we don't purge the evil, God will send events that will cleanse it for us. Situations will arise that push us to the edge and suddenly make us recall our mission or put issues into focus. This was demonstrated with a woman named Holly who suffered serious complications during surgery to correct a spinal syndrome. She bled, her lungs filled with fluid, and she lapsed into pulmonary edema. While she was in critical condition, she seemed to "slip" to the other side, and Jesus started speaking to her.

She recovered, but three weeks later, she dislocated two discs in her neck.

"The pain was terrible and nothing could control it," she recalled. "Here I was in horrible shape again looking at cervical fusion surgery. I felt so abandoned. It took time for me to realize that I had not been abandoned at all. I was being given a reminder. I had been treated to a special gift. I had lived through it and had forced myself to forget about it as soon as it was over. I had not learned my lesson. What lesson? The lesson that I should share my experience and not be ashamed of it. I should use my gift the best I could to assure others that death is not really something to be feared."

Hidden in all of our lives are failed missions. It is the soul's sense of an incomplete mission that causes fear of death. We are not ready. Such failings must be purged, especially direct transgressions. Spirits enter our existence when we sin, and then set out to plague us. Once open to them, we may find ourselves susceptible to mood swings.

Demons attach to our emotions. They aggravate us. If we have unhealed emotional wounds, they irritate those also. Mostly, they magnify negativity, which serves to negate the miraculous.

One of the great needs in the modern Church is a return to the practice of deliverance. Around the world, thousands suffer from demonic problems that are ignored, misdiagnosed, or discarded because in many dioceses, there isn't even an exorcist.

Satan likes this. He is an angel of the dark, and operates with stealth. Most of the time, we don't realize he is affecting us. Strange as it may seem, demons have certain legal rights, and one is to hover over "dedicated" territory. When evil is done, that person or place or thing is "dedicated" to the dark spirit until that spirit is purged. This is why we find phenomena occurring in certain parts of the country where there were pagan rites; the land has been dedicated to them.

Near Lake Helen, Florida, is an area that has been plagued by misfortunes of all kinds. There have been bizarre homicides, and the highways in the area are tremendously hazardous – the scene, in the words of one newspaper, of "hellacious" accidents. In one case, three separate fatal accidents occurred in the span of just a week, all within miles of that locale, which is also known for old Indian rituals (there is a mound nearby) and a camp for spirit mediums.

It is well-documented in the literature of exorcists: when we have something that connects with a source that is demonic, an evil energy may well hover around us. I have often seen cases where illicit sex, the use of drugs, crime, and the occult have drawn unwelcome spirits into a home. This can cause everything from anxiety, oppression, and other emotional upsets to actual physical discomfort (for example headaches, insomnia, and digestive disorders). In strong cases, things go bump in the night.

Often, it comes through objects. Books can carry an actual spiritual attachment, as can pictures, magazines, photographs, or computer files. It doesn't have to be occult. It can also be a connection to drugs, violence, or pornography. If you have such items in your homes, purge them. They will cause spiritual blockage. If you have books about the occult (witchcraft, satanism, astrology, New Age, psychics, mediums, vampires, horror thrillers) or books by or about evil people (especially murderers), these can bring an energy into your home because in reading it you have established a dark connection.

Prayer, fasting, and Communion are effective means of purging such evil and establishing protection. The one who prays is not afraid of the future and the one who fasts is not afraid of evil. There has been a correlation between the halt in fasting and the rise of the devil. Without fasting, evil easily penetrates. The doors of protection are left open. When we fast, we leave more room for God and become more spiritually sensitive. Fasting is like a spiritual insurance policy. Whoever fasts and abandons himself to

God does not have room in the heart for anguish. Difficulties will arise, but they will serve for spiritual growth and render God glory. When we act with humility and trust, Satan is bound. To fast is to cure because to fast is to cleanse. If you pray and fast, you will know what to request and you will obtain it. There will be miraculous cures. "These demons can only be cast out through prayer and fasting," says *Matthew* 17:21.

Misfortunes are frequently sent to remind us that we have strayed or forgotten something. The results are often astonishing – a purging of evil will cause a miraculous change in a person's life. Are there rooms in your home where rancor seems especially prevalent? Use Holy Water and blessed salt to clear the air.

Every time you sin, or feel anger, anytime you do not forgive, you give the devil a foothold. Every moment is laid out (see *Psalm* 139:16), and we are supposed to use every moment to purge evil.

Chapter 35

God changes our plans because He has a better one

When we do, a whole new life opens before us. Evil must be approached with discipline. In this way do we grow. And in this way does the Lord groom us.

"Every branch that bears fruit, He prunes it so that it may bear more fruit," says *John* 15. "You are already clean because of the Word which I have spoken to you. Abide in Me, and I in you. As the branch cannot bear fruit of itself unless it abides in the vine, so neither can you unless you abide in Me. I am the vine, you are the branches; he who abides in Me and I in him, he bears much fruit, for apart from Me you can do nothing."

Suffering is God pruning us to make us more productive.

After difficulty comes clarity and often purity of intention.

When things go differently than we planned, it's because God may have a hidden design that will bear more fruit than our own plan. In fact I'm sure of this. Here I recall the account of a woman named Edith who was heartbroken after a pet parakeet got loose. "She had the little bird trained to sit on her shoulder and smother her with kisses," a friend of hers wrote to me from Queens, New York. "There was no mistake that this was truly a love affair. But on a bitterly damp December afternoon, Edith was shaking out a rug by the front stoop, the door open, and she forgot that she had the bird perched outside its cage. Suddenly the parakeet tried to fly onto her shoulder and Edith became alarmed. Not realizing it was the bird, she jolted in surprise. The bird became frightened and flew into the sky. Edith tried desperately to call it back, but to no avail. She recruited a female passerby who tried to help her search for the bird. A half an hour later, a neighbor suggested that she put the cage outside with food hoping the bird may see it and enter. As soon as Edith set it outside, a yellow parakeet flew in! Everyone was amazed; yet Edith could not really rejoice because she worried about her own little bird lost out in the cold...

"Anyway, after a lengthy search, she rang my front door. I stepped out, knowing something was wrong by the expression on her face. She relayed the bittersweet story. As Edith was talking, I was strongly lured to look both to my immediate left and my immediate right. As I did, I saw one single beautiful yellow rose in bloom on a bush in the neighbor's yard and a single deep pink rose directly to the right in the yard of my other neighbor. I had a sudden urge to pray to St. Therese the Little Flower and I assured Edith she would find her bird, gave her a hug, and went inside. I proceeded to pray with all my heart almost feeling that this would be a reality.

"Two days later, Edith came by almost breathless with joy! Somehow, that day, she said, the passerby who initially tried to help her find the bird spotted a notice on the bulletin board of a local store stating that a blue parakeet was found and that the owner should contact them immediately. She quickly left to find Edith. She was not sure where Edith lived as she approached our section of the neighborhood. My husband was working out in our front yard and overheard her ask a neighbor if he knew where the woman was who lost her bird lived. Hearing this, my husband proceeded to show her Edith's house around the corner. Edith called the people who found her bird and found out that they were her friends from the local parish! I knew them too, since we all attended the same parish, often seeing each other at daily Mass."

Edith was full of thankfulness. "She regained her Christmas spirit and *more,* for now she has double the blessings: two birds for the crisis of one! I told her how I had prayed to St. Therese, and she suddenly turned white. Apparently that was her confirmation name! Indeed, God needed to find a special home for the lost yellow bird in the cold and began a special plan to do it. Not only should this remind us that apparent tragedies can actually turn out to be blessings, but also that God does look after the birds of the air and therefore, promises even more so to keep us in His care. I am convinced that He definitely has every hair on our heads counted!"

Let me mention my own story of how God changes our plans because He has a better one. When we were ready to move to Florida, we had our hearts set on the gorgeous city of St. Augustine, but my in-laws couldn't find a home there. Instead of feeling devastated, we prayed and the Holy Spirit led us to a town we never heard of south of St. Augustine. We got there in a thick fog that lifted when we walked out of early Sunday Mass – and there before us was a brand new community more attractive and yet far less expensive than the homes we had seen in St. Augustine with a Catholic school that perfectly fit the bill for our children. It turned out to be a far better place for a young family – lush, full of kids, and not far from the ocean!

Chapter 36

The prayer of 'desperation'

Bear fruit, and do it by not giving up. You can never pray too much. That will lead you to His plan.

"The seed is the word of God," the Bible tells us. "Those on the path are the ones who have heard, but the devil comes and takes away the word from their hearts that they may not believe and be saved. Those on rocky ground are the ones who, when they hear, receive the word with joy, but they have no root; they believe only for a time and fall away in time of temptation. As for the seed that fell among thorns, they are the ones who have heard, but as they go along, they are choked by the anxieties and riches and pleasures of life, and they fail to produce mature fruit. But as for the seed that fell on rich soil, they are the ones who, when they have heard the word, embrace it with a generous and good heart, and bear fruit through perseverance."

We must always endure through temptations, trials, and suffering. And we must keep steadfast in prayer. God sees prayers of perseverance as a light and is drawn to it. One woman who had a near-death episode said that on the other side she saw "many lights shooting up from the earth like beacons.

"Some were very broad and charged into Heaven like broad laser beams," she wrote. "Others resembled the illumination of small pen lights, and some were mere sparks."

The larger prayers, she explained, were those said with great faith from the heart (prayers of real desire), while the tiniest ones were no doubt prayers said of unfelt repetition.

Believe with an ever-living faith. Hope beyond hope.

The greatest prayers, she was told, were those that were unselfish and persistent. She saw angels answering each prayer in turn. "I was distinctly told that all prayers of desire are heard and answered," wrote this woman. "When we have great need, or when we are praying for other people, the beams project straight from us and are immediately visible. I was also told that there is no greater prayer than that of a mother for her children. These are the purest prayers because of their intense desire and, at the same time, sense of desperation. A mother has the ability to give her heart to her children and to implore mightily before God for them. We all have the ability, however, to reach God with our prayers. I understood that once our prayers of desire have been released, we need to let go of them and trust in the power of God to answer them."

It is what I have called the "prayer of desperation" and I am reminded of a woman in Connecticut with twin boys, boys who later became U.S. Marines. She had a devotion to the Rosary, and raised them as "religiously" as she could, praying constantly for them. Their names are Joseph and Rocco Nasiatka, and like others their age, they fell from the faith as they became burly young men.

Rocco ended up in Viet Nam as a machine gunner and had a deep foreboding that he was going to die. Friends felt the same way. It was that inner "knowing." Back at home his mother was praying.

Rocco was based with Delta Company, first battalion, Seventh Marines and one night at the end of June in 1968 as he was stationed on an ambush, at what was called Hill 41 (watching for the enemy as others slept), operating an M-60 machine gun, a woman he identified as the Blessed Mother was suddenly before him — hovering directly in front of his gun sights. He may have shaken his head, he may have blinked to make sure he was not awake, but there was no doubting it. It was like something he would have imagined.

She was dressed in blue and elevated off the ground and she explained to him that in the "stream of life" — the plan that had been organized for Rocco — it had been determined that he would end his life journey in the war.

"I was to die in Viet Nam," says Rocco. "I had felt that — I had felt before I left for Viet Nam that I had been marked for death, and others worried about this too — but I still did it because it was my duty. I was a Marine." Now it was confirmed to him: he was to die there.

But that outcome, said the woman, had been "mitigated," and instead, the Blessed Mother announced, he was being given the alternative of taking on a suffering.

Rocco agreed as long as it was not an injury to his head, and the apparition pointed cryptically to her hand.

Could it really be true? An ephemeral woman before him!

A week later, while on night ambush on July 4, 1968, Rocco had rested his hand atop the machinegun's "feed cover" when his unit was suddenly fired upon. It was a surprise attack and it fulfilled the prophecy. Four bullets ravaged Rocco's left hand while another hit between the fingers of his right. But the position of the left hand was just enough to deflect the bullets from striking his head!

"When the Holy Mother talked to me, she'd said it would be my left index finger that would be amputated, and what they did was take a good portion of my hand because gangrene set in," Rocco recalls. "They did take the finger off, too. But the one on the right hand, if you could see it, you'd wonder how it could happen. It went through the skin and didn't hit a bone, a pure miracle, plain and simple!"

Meanwhile, Joseph was a sergeant who served in Guam, and as it happens, he *too* would see Mary. That occurred 27 years later, when she appeared out of the blue — once again was just *there* – while Joseph was praying in his bedroom. When she arrived, says Joseph, all else — everything in the room — disappeared.

"It was September 1995," he says. "I had been a military policeman, and so I took in a lot of details. She looked about 25 years of age, very beautiful, very small stature. She wasn't large. And she was barefoot. She had like a blue shawl and I asked her, point blank, 'why did you intervene for my brother,' because I remembered that she had seen my brother in Viet Nam — and she said, *'It was your mother's tears and prayers that had gotten my attention.'* I asked her to explain to me why that would happen, and she made a gesture with her hands. She said, *'In life there's a life stream.'* She said, *'Your brother was to die in Viet Nam.'* That's what she said. And she added, *'I asked the Father for mercy, and mercy was granted.'*"

The prayers of a mother, over the course of years — prayer from the heart, of desire — had staved off tragedy. Such prayers spawned during our own spiritual "pruning" accumulate and come into use when their time comes. The same was testified to by a flight attendant named Beverly Raposa who was on an Eastern Airlines jumbo jet that famously crashed in the Everglades in the 1970s. During what experts later saw as an "unsurvivable" crash, Beverly was spared while the flight attendants across and in front of her died. She attributed her survival to a devotion in which one goes to Mass, adores the Blessed Sacrament on the first Friday, recites an act of consecration to the Sacred Heart, and states a prayer of reparation. It's the First Friday devotion. *"I promise thee in the excessive mercy of My Heart that My all-powerful love will grant to all those who communicate on the First Friday in nine consecutive months, the grace of final penitence,"* Jesus once told a saint named Margaret Mary Alacoque. *"They shall not die in My disgrace nor without receiving the Sacraments; My Divine heart shall be their safe refuge in this last moment."*

Even though she had strayed from her faith, Beverly is convinced this devotion came back to help her in that darkest and most terrifying of moments.

"I believe that because I had made the nine First Fridays in high school and truly believed in His promises, that I was saved, as I was not in a state of grace that night," stated the former flight attendant. "The emergency chute on the back rear door inflated over me, stopping at a point that continuing on would have smothered me. I fell through the floor with 400 pounds on top of me, but the chute protected me. As a new flight attendant I had purchased a statue of Our Lady at the chapel at JFK Airport. She was standing on a propeller and had the left side of her mantle out. On the mantle was a jet plane! Is there any doubt that her mantle — the chute — protected me, and I lived because of one of the First Friday promises.... *'you shall not die in my disgrace'?"*

Chapter 37

Faith without love is vain

When we pray, we are never wasting time, unless the prayer is totally self-centered. And no matter what we fear, prayer offers a buffer. This works by following the biblical admonishment to pray without ceasing. At the very least, all day, we can utter, *"Jesus. Jesus."* In His Name, we may also invoke saints. As much as the Lord connects us with other people, so too does he connect us with spiritual helpers on the other side. If a set of books were written to include every miracle performed during the past 2,000 years at the behest of a saint, the books would fill a New York skyscraper. I have seen this countless times, and it only makes sense: if we can request the prayers of those living, why not also those who are deceased and who are closer to God, Who can see Him?

The more merit they have, the stronger their intercession. Endless are the accounts of signs from the other side – little items that mysteriously show up to remind the living that saints exist, or dreams in which the veil is parted, if fleetingly. When favors are granted, we may suddenly come across the picture of someone we knew who may well have intervened for us. A friend of mine was known for roses, and when she died, rose petals or their fragrance suddenly began appearing in improbable ways, including next to the altar after a priest had given a memorial talk about her (even though the church had no flowers). Petals also appeared to a mourning daughter.

The major saints grant large signs. One case that came to my attention involved a Worcester, Massachusetts, businessman named Daniel O'Malley whose wife was given an oyster shell from a Protestant who found it at a park in Vero Beach, Florida. The shell bears a startling resemblance to classic depictions of the Virgin Mary, defined even to the robe and more impressive was the effect: it led Daniel, who carried bitterness over the loss of a child, back to the Church and even took him to daily devotion. The root of all this seemed to be his mother — who lived in Florida and died several years before (a devout woman who was dedicated to Mary, the Rosary, and St. Anthony, the patron of things found)! "I have no doubt about it," says Dan of the role he now believes his mother plays from Heaven.

The seashell joins other objects like tree trunks or rocks that seem to have images of Jesus or Mary in them, at least for many who see them that way. In Boston, there was the image of Mary on a hospital window, while in Florida a stunningly detailed resemblance of her formed in the oxidation of reflective glass on an office, which I have mentioned. Some of it may be in the mind of the beholder, but such reports are not to be dismissed out of hand. Everything physical comes from the supernatural, and the supernatural inflects itself at strategic times. Moreover, nothing that God does is frivolous. It was through such miraculous signs that the early Church was formed, with chapels built to commemorate manifestations. Few realize that it was appearances by the Blessed Mother, or phenomena occurring with statues, that served as the inspiration for countless churches from the very first century. The same occurs with light. I have many photographs of extraordinary formations of light, usually from the sun, as God easily manipulates His Creation.

Such are granted to bolster our faith and perseverance. They are communicated from the other side. Today thousands of statues have wept tears or exuded an oily substance. In some cases, Church-appointed experts have closely analyzed the situations and have determined that there is no natural explanation. Tests frequently show it to be olive oil. Often it heals. I myself have held an object as oil emanated from it. In Italy, this happened to a bishop. In Australia, a priest whose church was the site of several alleged miracles told parishioners that his personal rosary beads shed oil at the same time that oil was flowing from a portrait of Jesus.

God is the God of nature and can inflect His signs into the entire spectrum of physicality. Shortly before September 11, the formation of sap in a tree in Upper Manhattan uncannily resembled a weeping Mary. Did that qualify as a manifestation?

In other cases, the intervention is far more direct. This is especially true with saints.

"In 1981, when I was 26 years old, I was captured by the British Army and thrown into Crumlin Road Jail, Belfast, in the North of Ireland," a man named Padraig Caughey wrote me. "At the time I was extremely bitter and full of hate, not believing in God at all and very angry at the Catholic Church which I considered to be pro-British. But the years of rage and violence during the 'Troubles' had taken their toll on me and I was increasingly suicidal. The only thing that stopped me from killing myself was the knowledge that it would bring great pain to my family.

"One night as I entered my cell I found a newspaper photo of St. Padre Pio bearing his stigmata lying on the floor. I don't know how it got there as neither myself or my cell-mate were believers. Anyway as I looked at the marks of the passion on Padre Pio's hands, I thought, 'He did it with a screwdriver!' But I wondered how he had never gotten blood poisoning nor been caught cheating over such a long life.

"That night as I was going to sleep, I said in despair, 'Padre Pio, go to God and ask Him to prove to me He really exists in the space of one *Hail Mary,* for if He doesn't I will know for certain that He does not exist and I can go ahead and kill myself.'

"As soon as I said 'Hail Mary,' my eyes flooded with tears in rivers, for there standing at the end of the bed in great glory was the Mother of God herself. Extraordinary holiness, and beauty, and majesty, and motherliness, and love, and kindness; indescribable!! She said, *'Now you believe?'* I could only nod and say, 'Yes, I believe!' Then she said, *'Faith without love is vain. You must forgive; do you forgive?'*

"Then I saw before me picture forms of all who I had hated, while Mary's voice gently kept asking me, *'Do you forgive, do you forgive, do you forgive, ...'* as each one passed before me. Then she said, *'Now is there anyone, anyone at all, to whom you bear hate?'*

"There was no-one; I forgave them all; it was as though the weight of the universe was lifted from my soul. For the first time Mary smiled. *"Now you have faith and now you have loved; now you must pray, for prayer is the food of faith. Pray, pray the Rosary,'* she said, and she held a set of beads towards me. I was embarrassed and said, 'I am sorry I have forgotten how to say them.' Mary said with great firmness, *'I myself will teach you!'* And she was gone. I cannot tell the joy I felt; it was as though I was reborn. I found it hard to say the Rosary at first, but then I came to love it. Eventually I ended up saying it all the time. The way Mary taught it was not at all as we prayed it as a child. It was slow and thoughtful. When I left prison, I entered a Cistercian Monastery."

Chapter 38

Only in His Name do we pray

As for the ordinary deceased, they too intercede, and let us know it. If you need help, ask those in both Heaven and purgatory.

They are always watching, and when we pray, the veil scrolls up, the veil that separates us.

Invoking Heaven is a major part of the miraculous life, as long as we are cautious not to wander into "mediumship" (initiating conversations with the other side, which can be demons in disguise), and as long as we remember that all power and glory comes from Jesus.

Only in His Name do we pray.

But pray we must, and to the angels, including warring ones.

Magnificent, giant, muscular spirits are in Heaven watching for our prayers, with a wonderful countenance about them.

What sets them apart is their total confidence.

They are certain of their abilities.

Nothing evil could daunt them. They know the importance of what they are doing, and they also know that they will not return until the mission is accomplished.

Teresa Brownlee of California can attest to that.

She relates a drama that involved her son.

At the time, she says, he was "on crack cocaine, very, very ill and dangerous."

Then came the incident. "He had weapons and was preparing to kill a doctor and his dealer when his wife called me and I raced at almost 100 miles per hour to get to them to help her," said Teresa.

"I went into a room where he was in the dark loading a very dangerous sawed-off shotgun and other weapons. I was horrified and began to pray over him when I felt something came out of him and swirl around me — the presence of evil, which was extremely strong. I had not gone to Mass that day (it was during the week and I work), and I was guided by the Holy Spirit to leave the room. The presence was so strong it almost knocked me over! Without the sacraments in me, I knew I had no weapons to go against this thing of evil.

"I had tried to pray over my son and he picked up the phone, ripped it out of the wall, and threw it against the wall to break it," Teresa continued. " I fled the room in tears and as my daughter-in-law was fleeing the house, dropped to my knees and begged God to please send St. Michael the Archangel and his army to stop my son! *I continually prayed* and pleaded with no knowledge of anything around me."

It was this persistence that worked the miracle.

"I stayed in prayer for about twenty minutes when all of a sudden, my son came out of the room and spoke in a gentle voice. 'I am ready to go to the hospital now,' he said. His wife came back in from the car and stood her ground and said, 'Are you sure? I will not put up with any more of your violence. I will call the police and there is the risk they will shoot you.' He affirmed that he would go in peace. His voice had completely changed! When she got him to the hospital, the director of Knollwood Hospital in Riverside asked him why he decided to come for help and he told him the following account: 'I was going to kill my dealer and a doctor who refused my help because of insurance difficulties. I am on days of crack cocaine. My mother tried to stop me and I even had thoughts to hurt her. But when she left the room, I tried to load my sawed-off [shotgun], and each time I approached the chamber with the bullet, it would fly out of my finger. I could not load the gun for anything! I felt a change come over me and gave up! That is why I am here!'"

"This all happened," interjected Teresa, "while I was on my knees begging Almighty God to send Saint Michael to stop him. The director of the hospital said, 'Well, that sounds like Divine intervention to me!' He was finally arrested and it was all on television. He is serving fifteen years in prison! But my prayers for his salvation are being answered. The journey is one of Calvary and the walk can be very difficult, after Jesus and His Mother, but oh how privileged we are to be able to walk behind them! I encourage all parents to pray, pray, and pray for their families. Never give up! The Lord hears our prayers. His mighty angels will assist us. "

When we pray, we draw close to God, and He grants an intervention that can not be attained elsewhere. Prayer, especially in times of despair and anguish, moves the Heart of God if offered, said John Paul II, with humility. What does Scripture tell us? "I was caught by the cords of death," says *Psalm* 114 , "the snares of Sheol had seized me; I felt agony and dread. Then I called on the name of the Lord, 'O Lord, save my life!'"

It is a brief but intense prayer of the man who, finding himself in a desperate situation, holds fast to the only real plank of salvation.

"Once saved, the person at prayer proclaims that the Lord is 'gracious and just,' more than that, 'merciful,'" noted John Paul II. "Genuine trust always sees God as love, even if at times it is difficult to understand his actions. It is certain, nevertheless, that 'The Lord protects the simple.' Therefore, in misery and abandonment, one can always count on him, 'Father of the fatherless, defender of widows.'"

Invoked with faith, the Lord extends His Hand, breaks the coils that encircle you, dries the tears from your eyes, and stops what might otherwise be a precipitous descent. "Prayer helps to discover the loving Face of God," said the Pope. "He never abandons His people but guarantees that, notwithstanding trials and suffering, in the end good triumphs."

When we have passed beyond the stages where sentiments, clarification, fears, preoccupation, immediate results, and easy achievements matter, noted a priest I know, then we understand what the mystery of faith is. Christ came to His disciples walking on water to share with them the powerful experience of being totally safe in the Father's embrace. Our religion is an eruption from an unseen force that was seen in Jesus. Because His disciples were satisfied with the mysterious, they could experience His peace.

God is always there when we let Him close and when we encounter the roaring seas in our lives. Let's face it: all of us will face crises. But if we could see with God's eyes, if we knew the full picture, we might see that in fact everyone faces equal tragedy. Many sufferings are not visible. But we all go through it. Try as we might, we never reach a perfect state (where everything goes our way). It may do so for a day or two, even a week, but usually a good day is followed by a test.

We are simply called to endure. We all die; there is eternity; life on earth is a test. If you were God and had watched all those angels rebel, you would also want to test. Why do disasters occur? I found it interesting when a priest, Father Joseph Lionel, from the one of the hardest hit areas in India in the wake of the tsunami, noted that "perhaps we can also view matters not so much as God punishing those victims specifically, as the fact that when sin builds in the world, it puts the world out of order. It causes an actual darkness that can physically — and geologically — manifest. Events come almost as a release of that dark tension. God allows it. The good suffer with the evil. There are victim souls and always have been."

Tempests arrive in our lives, and if a number of circumstances are in place, we can face a "perfect storm." That's when one unusually potent system interlocks with others. A frigid blast of Arctic air might collide with a system of wet snowmaking weather over the Atlantic and the result is a northeaster. We know that special circumstances of hot and cool air create cyclonic motion to spawn twisters. There are high and low pressure centers, and they interact.

So too do circumstances burst with turbulence in our own lives. Both mundane and spiritual forces converge. We may be at an especially tender emotional moment when a big hassle comes at work, accompanied by an argument with a spouse and trouble with our children, even serious trouble, such as drugs. The world seems to be crashing down. It's one thing after another. *And it is how we handle these "storms" that counts.* Crucial is taking them one at a time and remembering to step back without over-reacting. Wait for the wave to crest.

Like fear, over-reaction grants power to the devil. It is important to remember that a better day will follow, as indeed with faith in God it always does. If we have a "bank account" of prayers, and if we have sought closeness to God, He affords protection. During the New Orleans tragedy, many were those who felt His Hand; many prayed that the city would be spared a direct hit, and while a catastrophe followed, the worst of the hurricane was diverted at the last moment by a puff of dry air from the Midwest that was completely unexpected and caused the hurricane to decrease in intensity and turn slightly east.

A statue of Him in front of the famous cathedral in the French quarter miraculously survived save for the index finger and thumb that locals decided were symbols of how He had flicked the storm away.

He said there would be roaring waves (*Luke* 21:25-26); there would be storms in life. And fear is the obstacle to overcoming them. We saw this in the case of that tsunami. There were those who prayed and found themselves miraculously untouched even though the water seemed to crest over their heads, or as in the case of one missionary, an instance in which – upon his invoking of Jesus – a surge of water seemed to momentarily freeze at the mouth of a lagoon (allowing for his escape).

In both India and Sri Lanka, Catholic shrines saw little damage despite water roiling around them and destroying adjacent properties (at the same elevation).

That happened at the shrine of Vailankanni as well as at the Shrine of Our Lady of Matara, where the waves washed over a 500-year-old statue of Virgin and Child that was said to have miraculous powers and indeed it was later located in shorelines debris with no damage (the Infant was still wearing His crown). In the village of Batiagon, in the Jagatsinghpur District of India, there were just two buildings made of concrete: a church and a rich man's house, said reports. The rest of the buildings were straw and clay. People rushed into the two buildings for shelter. About 300 people, both Christians and non-Christians, jammed into the church and cried out for His protection. "At around 11 a.m., a massive tidal wave thirty feet high slammed into the village, instantly destroying the shacks and sweeping away the rich man's house," said the report of this. "Witnesses inside the church say the wave seemed to split and go around both sides of the building. All 300 people who had taken shelter inside the church survived.... All the people in Batiagon village confessed that God had graciously saved their lives. The Hindus declared they would never again oppose Christianity."

Chapter 39

Thankfulness works the miracle

God is our shield and when you draw nearer to Him, you draw nearer to a sense of well-being. It's that simple. There's nothing you can do that will bring as much protection. And closeness comes through praise. Adore God throughout the day. Do it from the heart. Love Him. Praise Him ten times, a hundred times. That's what will bring you joy, because the Lord is the personification of joy.

Jesus said we should request the favor of God (*Matthew* 7:7-9), knock at the "door," and this we must do, knowing that if something is good for us and in the plan of Christ, plus asked with faith, which means in a way that is fearless, it will be granted. Ask the Holy Spirit what it is you *should* ask for. And do it in the Name of Jesus. In this way, anything is possible. As we feel honored and close to those who appreciate us, so too is it with God: praise brings us closeness.

What we receive is often in direct proportion to our thankfulness. A priest ice fishing on a frozen Canadian lake, in one of those wood-heated portable shanties, wasn't having much luck. This was January 4, 2005, on Tobin Lake near Nipawin in northern Saskatchewan. His name was Father Mariusz Zajac, and it was just before 5 p.m. when, having put in a few hours of fishing, he resolved to call it a day. "I had a few nibbles but that was it, I didn't catch anything," said the Polish-born priest. But he added that before packing up, he decided to recite the Canticle of Mary — an evening prayer from the Gospel of Luke, which gives thanks to God for each day, despite the bad luck fishing. "On these words, I got a bite," he recalled. It was a 36-inch fish, 18-pound, the world record for walleye caught while ice fishing.

No matter what you may be going through — pain, depression, worries, frustration — if you praise God He will bring you to fruition. *Love Him more than you have ever loved anyone.* He brings joy where, by the standards of the world, there should be depression. He sends graces that defy our circumstances. There are those who are lonely. There are those in poverty. There are those with cancer. There are those with sons who are addicted to drugs. In God they trust and find gladness.

We should not thank Him thinking it is a magic formula in attaining what we want. There is no *abracadabbra*. God knows our true hearts, and we have to have hearts full of thankfulness – hearts that are in gratitude to Him whether or not He is responding to our requests. "Thank you, Jesus," we should say all the time. "Thank you Christ." Repeat it. Keep saying it. It lifts our hearts. Thank God, love Him, and watch Him draw nigh. "Oh give thanks to the Lord, call upon His name," says *1 Chronicles*.

"I will praise the name of God with song," it says in *Psalms*. "And magnify Him with thanksgiving."

"Always giving thanks," adds *Ephesians*, "for all things in the name of our Lord Jesus Christ to God, even the Father"!

Chapter 40

Turn fear into the energy of action

We'll be spending an eternity praising, adoring, and thanking God, and it's good to get practice. He is worthy of all worship and in our times we forget how long His mercy has endured and how we must thank him all the more intensely.

Ungratefulness and pride build walls that separate us from God while humility is the bridge to Heaven.

God illuminates with shafts of light and tapping into that brilliance is the key to the miraculous. That is an important message for our time: We live at a moment in history when science is trying to declaim anything that may be miraculous, and when even many in religious institutions have lost belief in such interventions (as if the Holy Spirit stopped shedding such grace 2,000 years ago), but actually Jesus told us upon His Ascension that He would be sending the Holy Spirit (not taking Him with Him), and it is the Holy Spirit Who works miracles. This is why it is important to constantly invoke the Spirit in the Name of Jesus.

I once spoke to an internationally known cancer surgeon named Dr. Michael H. Torosian who prays before every operation and says the results are often "remarkable."

Without prayer, he would be your standard surgeon.

Prayer affords the opportunity for the Holy Spirit to work within us — and He does so in many ways that are without explanation. Time and again I have seen miracles spring from faith if that faith is unwavering.

"A lot of physicians have a hard time grasping this because they're taught as scientists to 'prove' things and you can't prove a lot that goes on in the spiritual realm," noted Dr. Torosian. "But we see a lot of things that you can't explain with just physical data."

"Approximately one-third of the Gospel is taken up by the cures wrought by Jesus in the brief period of His public life," notes Father Raniero Cantalamessa, the preacher of the Pontifical Household in Rome. "It is impossible to eliminate these miracles, or to give them a natural explanation, without distorting the whole Gospel and making it incomprehensible."

One of the most astonishing cures happened to a doctor himself, Vinicio Arrieta, a Harvard-educated physician who was director of medicine at the University of Zulia in Venezuela. He experienced his healing at a holy spot near Caracas that stands as one of the few officially approved by the Catholic Church as a place where Mary has appeared in apparition. Originally owned by a Pentecostal and known as "Betania" (which means Bethany, where Jesus, as described in *Luke* 24, gave His famous blessing), it was later purchased by a Catholic mystic and that is how Dr. Arrieta, who was suffering from cancer of the prostate, heard of it.

He was in desperate need. The cancer had spread to the lumbar column of his spine. He had been given two years to live.

But Arrieta had not given up. Instead, he placed his faith in God and turned fear into the energy of action. He also cleared his conscience. He told the Lord – pleaded – that he wanted to live for his children, and renounced his pretentiousness.

After that confession, Dr. Arrieta spent all night praying, and at six in the morning, with others crowded there for a feast day, he sang a little song to the Blessed Mother. As he did, says Arrieta, the sun seemed to act strangely. The center became green and it also began to pulse, to spin on the inside, and to whirl closer, as during the famous apparitions at Fatima – which in fact was the feast day the pilgrims there were commemorating.

"I began to feel an infusion, a heat within my body," recalled Dr. Arrieta. "I grabbed my wife, and I began to scream, 'I'm being cured! I'm being cured! I'm being cured!' They thought I was crazy. But I felt this infusion arrive at my spinal column and go to my prostate."

At that point the doctor claims he himself saw an apparition of the Virgin, shedding grace as in classic portraits such as the Miraculous Medal.

"Five days later," he adds, "the prostatic specific antigen indicating the cancer was not detectable."

Chapter 41

We overcome when we persevere

I have other accounts from doctors, and I have many accounts of the sun acting strangely, which seems to be a special miracle of our own time. God can inflect whatever image He wants to impress into our consciousness. In Dr. Arrieta's case, 5,000 others witnessed the phenomenon, and I myself have seen the miracle of the sun on three continents. We live in extraordinary times and should take advantage of the extraordinary grace.

More often than not, such grace comes in a way that is subtle and occurs over time. It is important for us to do likewise and not force things but nurture goodness along. God shows us this in nature. He has designed it so that it can take more than a generation for a single olive tree to bear fruit, but once it does, it does so for centuries.

The same holds true for us: our lives should be lived in a way that takes one thing at a time. We should not "gulp" it all down, we should not rush-rush through, and our patience should come from the recognition of God's timing. Many healings are so gradual that we never see them as miracles. As the Pontifical preacher said, "miracles of the Gospel present unmistakable characteristics. They were never carried out to astonish or extol the one working them. There are some today who allow themselves to be fascinated when listening to those who seem to have certain powers of levitation, of making things appear and disappear, and other such things."

That can tend toward the occult, and occult miracles are dangerous. In the end, when the "energy" comes from the wrong source, it causes more harm than good; when the devil heals, it is temporary and something worse is suffered in exchange.

Evil begins when we go the way of magic, which exerts pressure from alleged occult powers of the person and as the preacher said, "are not based either on science or faith. In this case, either we are before charlatanism and deceit, or worse, the action of the enemy." We can tell those who may be false by the fact that the focus is on *them*. It is also a bad sign when money is involved. Jesus worked miracles out of compassion because He loved people. He also did it to help them believe. He healed to proclaim that God is the Lord of life and that in the end, together with death, sickness will be overcome, if we persevere.

As St. Hildegarde said, our bodies are "vivified" by the Spirit. It permeates our veins, the marrow of our bones, and the juice of our flesh. It is this force that coordinates our physical existence and it's this force that organizes an incredibly complex biological system which certainly wasn't created by chance.

The theory of evolution (which means an "unfolding") has been hijacked by those who believe this "unfolding" took place not by way of supernatural design, but by natural selection – that random mutations in the genes led to physical traits that either made an organism superior to the rest and better able to survive, or caused it to die out.

The problem is that there are thousands of complicated interactions in the body and they go far beyond what could have occurred due to any random process in even a single simple organism, let alone thousands of complex species. There are millions of coordinated interactions in the body and they could not possibly be a fluke.

There are no accidents of nature. They are overseen by Spirit. Consider the camel's hump, essential for storage of water on the desert, or the way a chameleon lizard can switch color. Contemplate the platypus (there is no genetic line it seems to have derived from), and the actual light that some fish emit in the deepest part of the ocean (to lure fish or illuminate their surroundings). The black angler fish has a luminous forked structure on the roof of its mouth while a species of lantern fish has a light on its tongue. Coincidence?

It is the Spirit that organizes our organisms and it is tapping into the Spirit that thus causes healings.

Once more we turn to St. Hildegarde. "When by the mysterious order established by the Supreme Creator the body is quickened in the mother's womb, the soul like a fiery globe bearing no resemblance to the human form takes possession of the heart, mounts to the brain, and animates all members," said this great saint. "It gives strength to the heart which as the fundamental part governs the whole body, and like the firmament of Heaven holds together what is below it, hides what is above. It mounts to the brain, because in the wisdom of God it has the power to understand not only what is earthly, but also what is heavenly. It diffuses itself through all the members because it communicates vital strength to the whole body, to the marrow, the veins, to all the different parts just as a tree transmits sap from its roots to its branches that they may clothe themselves with leaves."

Here we see how God heals! These forces are His. The soul dwells in the heart – and so we see how we need to cleanse our hearts if we want to take advantage of the power behind it. Many sicknesses start here. It is where we are "wounded." It is also where hatred and unforgiveness can fester. The hurts from others linger as long as unforgiveness lingers — blocking connection with the higher force.

We see the nature of that force and God's desire to heal us even with the many reports of statues and other holy items that have shed or "wept" oil – the ancient balm of healing.

Many are those who oppose the use of statues in the belief that such devotion (praying with the aid of a visible representation) contravenes the Bible's admonishment not to make "graven images." Such concerns can be laid to rest. The biblical warning is in the context of pagan worship, the glorification of gods, goddesses, and even animals like the snake, which in biblical times were rampant from Rome to Babylon.

Those were not Christian images but demigods, and we note the passage in Scripture whereby the Holy Spirit directed Moses to build the Ark of the Covenant with the images of angels – indicating for sure that there is nothing wrong with holy art, as long as it points to Him.

"You shall make two cherubim of gold, make them of hammered work at the two ends of the mercy seat," the Lord said in *Exodus* 25, and since the time of Christ we have had a visible representation of God.

Images visually convey the Gospel message.

It is good to have a memento of what is holy (just as it is okay to have a photograph of a loved one) as long as we do not become obsessed with it. Any unusual attachment is of darkness. A woman named Erinn Elizabeth Moss of Nova Scotia who had been in pain for years due to a congenitally dislocated hip, necessitating the use of a cane or wheelchair, told me of a wondrous effect when she was visiting a pilgrim site with a large corpus of Christ. The corpus (the Body of Jesus Crucified, without the cross) exuded a mysterious flow in a way that baffled experts. The exudation, a cross between oil and water, has materialized for years from a bruised part of the knee of Jesus.

"We had all been rubbing our cloths or Kleenex on the statue, and I had done that as well," said Mrs. Moss. "I had a blue scarf from the tour group and two drops appeared. One evaporated as soon as I touched it and the other *began to turn red in front of our eyes* with a few droplets below it. It was amazing. It was like a splash mark nearly the size of a dime. We showed the Franciscans [including a priest who oversees English-speaking pilgrims] and he said it was an amazing gift. He said it was like the blood and water at the Crucifixion."

Erinn added that during the same trip she was inexplicably able to ascend the holy mountain there, which is topped by a Cross. "There was no way I thought I could climb Cross Mountain," she told me. "I went there and all of a sudden my hip shifted twice and I was able to go up as fast as anyone. I went up with a cane and I didn't need it. For 24 years I had pain and it stopped."

I spoke with a second woman named Rosalind Soares from Thorn Hill, Ontario, who rubbed a piece of pure white cloth on the knee of the statue, collecting the moisture in that fashion before it too disappeared. She also touched a statue of the Madonna to the fluid. "It just came down halfway down and evaporated," said Rosalind. "The drops never touched the ground. Sometimes three or four drops would come, then just one. When we went back, we said our prayers and I took my statue and put it on the knee where the water was exuding and sat down. I had the statue in my left hand and my rosary in my right hand and suddenly I felt a dampness in the palm of my hand and removed the statue to see what the feeling in my palm was. And my goodness, it was all red, like blood. There was quite a bit in the center of my palm! It wasn't rust. It was a beautiful, royal red, like a velvety liquid."

Thousands of statues elsewhere in the world have baffled witnesses.

In ways we don't comprehend, God delivers miracles to bolster us and sometimes causes them to proliferate. This was seen in Virginia with a priest named James Bruse, whose very presence seemed to cause statues to weep.

The phenomena began on November 28, 1991, when droplets of water welled in the eyes of a statue in the home of Father Bruse's parents. Soon, dozens of other statues shed tears, and thousands saw them. At one point, a statue wept in the bishop's office. It had started at a point in his life when Father Bruse, a young priest, began to question whether he should be a priest at all. He had little doubt after.

A bishop in Italy also held a statue as it wept, and a panel of experts declared that there was no natural explanation for what had happened.

Tears are the language that we understand best and it is only natural that Heaven would thus communicate with us in that fashion. These are miracles that touch the heart, and love is behind them. Love heals. It is the ointment of life, just as oil is a physical ointment. It gravitates to us when we have purity of intentions.

The last I knew an icon of the Virgin and Child continued to exude oil on a daily basis at a church in Livonia, Michigan, according to the pastor, Father Michael Matsko, of Holy Transfiguration Orthodox Church, who said there have been healings associated with this oil too — which has the aroma of myrrh and seems particularly to help childless women have children.

"There have been ten or 12 cases of women who had trouble having babies," the priest related. "We've had all kinds of miracles take place, from cancerous tumors being removed to the childless couples, but the most striking thing is the spiritual healing that takes place. There was a 17-year-old boy who came every week and died of his cancer, but he was prepared spiritually to enter the next world, knowing that God loves him and his soul was saved. That was moving. He had no fear."

This is the lesson of miracles, and reports of them come from around the world. Israel. Venezuela. Australia. A former monk in Kansas has reported thousands of medals, rosaries, statues, and prayer cards that have emanated a slight but mysterious oily sheen that, he says, has led to healing. Good fruits. One especially poignant case came from a nurse named Olivia Smith in Petrolia, Pennsylvania.

"On March 27, 2004, I went to St. Anthony's Chapel in Troy Hill, Pittsburgh, to meet with a prayer group that prays for priests from 10 a.m. until 1:00 p.m.," Olivia testified. "The staff at the chapel was gingerly cleaning the Stations of the Cross. They are life-sized and this is a big undertaking. The priest was most kind and merciful in the confessional. When I came to my seat after, the prayer group had started the Joyful Mysteries of the Rosary. This was one of the twenty decades we would pray that day. We were in front of the Most Holy Blessed Sacrament. While praying I looked down at wooden rosary beads and noticed that the beads were wet. I questioned what I witnessed and rubbed the rosary against paper — wondering if my eyes were fooling me. I touched the beads and felt the oil between my fingers — yet no oil came off on my hands or on the paper which I tried to blot it with! On the way home I prayed the Rosary and looked down in my hand. The beads were glistening. Wet. I thought of Our Lady's tears and Our Lord's sweat. His Mercy. His Blood. I was amazed. I'm fortunate I didn't rear-end the motorcycle in front of me! I told one of my closest friends, Rita, about the phenomenon. We prayed the Rosary and had benediction and Adoration. Rita brought her rosary. I gave her mine. Both rosaries had oil on the beads!'"

As overwhelmed and attached to the rosary as she was, Olivia was soon to lose it, and therein was the greater lesson. As it happens, that week she went to a nursing home for a prayer group and one of the residents asked if Olivia could spare a rosary – specifically, a wooden rosary — for a man who was thinking of becoming a priest. "I said, 'I'll get you one, but I can't give you this one," said Olivia. "It's miraculous." Mass began, and it was a beautiful. But before the sign of peace, Olivia heard a thought: *"You know, you have to give Betty that rosary."* Mentally, Olivia responded, "I can't. It's a miracle." And the voice continued, *"When someone asks you for a rosary, you must give it away. It will be a long time before you see her again. And besides she wants to give it to someone who wants to be a priest. Give her the rosary."*

"I weakly bandied with these thoughts and at the sign of peace, walked over to Betty," Olivia recalls. "I whispered, 'This is for that man. I hope he becomes a very good priest. This rosary is blessed; there is oil on the beads.' I pressed it into her hands and knelt down again and these big tears were rolling out of my eyes. It was a very beautiful Mass, and Mass can make you cry. So can giving away a treasure from God."

When Olivia got home, she left a message with Rita, telling her that she had given the miraculous rosary away. She and her friend had sent money to a woman who was going on pilgrimage. As it turns out, she brought back about 150 rosaries, made of wood.

Olivia was at work, praying for the sick, when the beads of one rosary suddenly became wet!

Soon the others likewise exuded a mysterious substance. One miracle had turned into dozens.

"I placed the rosaries on a table and they became wet at times as if they were perspiring," she recalls. "Very amazing. They were drenched, not dripping — just wet and glistening with oil!"

Chapter 42

Let go and let God

The more we give, the more we get, the message seemed to be — as long as we're not expecting anything in return.

Miracles can be multiplied in our own lives. The trigger is selflessness. When we are positive, the spiritual world is energized for action. What miracle cannot occur? What can't God do?

There are even cases of people who through prayer have been brought back from the dead.

There's the account of Li Peng. On the evening of January 8, 2004, according to news reports, he was swimming with a friend in a pool at an apartment complex in Saanich, British Colombia. They were alone with no lifeguard and Li, 19 at the time, "drowned," sinking to the bottom of the pool as the other dashed frantically for help.

That help took four minutes to arrive and despite attempts at resuscitation, Lin didn't regain consciousness.

An ambulance took him to the hospital with the bleakest of prognoses. "I probably would have said this is a non-survivable situation," noted a doctor. "Certainly, that's how my colleagues felt. I think it is fair to say that nursing and medical expectations for Li Peng were death or vegetative state."

Medical staff generally expect that if there are going to be any signs of recovery, they will occur in the first 72 hours. "But in Li's case, he was in deep coma and his condition appeared to be worsening by the day," noted a newspaper.

As the week progressed, they nearly halted his care. His father struggled to cope. Someone remembered a man from a Christian Chinese church, and he was summoned because he spoke a dialect Li's father could understand. It was a stroke of good "luck," for while the initial prayers didn't work, a subsequent prayer session led to the man's miraculous recovery. "We have no natural way of being able to understand why Li Peng gained what he did," said the doctor.

Li regained consciousness and full health. It was nearly like Lazarus. In some cases, it *is* like Lazarus. Axel Fischer, leader of a mission agency in Ulaanbaatar, Mongolia, reports that two people were raised from the "dead." "In both cases, the person had died in the hospital, and their deaths and resurrections were confirmed by doctors," he was quoted as saying on the internet. "Naraa, a Mongolian Christian who we have known for years, reports: 'One night, the desperate relatives of a man who had recently died asked us to come to the hospital. There are no doctors in our area, so we are often called on to pray for the sick. God has healed many people. I know that my God performs miracles, so I went to pray for the dead man, who was already cold when I arrived. After five minutes of prayer, he opened his eyes. His resurrection was the talk of the village. All the relatives gave their lives to Christ on the spot.' Badulzi, a pastor and close friend, told us the following: 'A young girl in our church died, but her Christian friends didn't want to accept her death. They believed that God could do wonders, so they prayed and praised God at her bedside for ten hours, until she returned to life. The doctors and other witnesses were astonished and could hardly comprehend that Jesus is also Lord over life and death.'"

Dozens of cases have been reported elsewhere. Just now across my desk comes the account of a toddler who was clinically dead for nearly two hours yet recovered. He had not taken a breath for 105 minutes! "I am astounded – I still can't explain it," said Dr. Andrew Numa, senior intensive care specialist at Children's Hospital in Sydney, Australia. A man named Larry Green was pronounced dead in North Carolina and placed in a body bag before he came back to life (due to prayer, say his relatives).

Many are those who have near-death brushes and say that they were pulled back by the prayers of relatives.

What about those who go even farther into the "hereafter"?

Those who have near-death experiences often describe a trip through a tunnel that seems to transport them through outer space amid strange lights.

Is this the cosmos?

Often they are met by deceased loved ones, or by angels. Most often it is a light that they identify as Jesus.

Before they progress further, like Storm, they are shown their lives. And like Storm, they see themselves in an entirely new perspective.

In that life review, when our own time comes, will be the secrets to every event we have experienced and every person we have met.

We could go on with the extraordinary lessons gained with such a perspective. They lead to questions we should ask ourselves in prayer every day: What have I done today that was unselfish? Whom have I helped?

Did I think of God? Did I add to the dignity of another person? How was I humble? How was I not humble? Whom did I love? Who didn't I love?

Ask yourself those questions because when you die they are among the questions you will be asked as you realize that every single minute of your life bore opportunity for advancement and hidden meaning.

Are you balanced? Too little water hurts a plant. So does too much. Do you go to extremes? By our fruits we will know ourselves, as well as others.

On our way to that balance God sends us signs to point us in the right direction. Most are small – the little miracles. We take full advantage of them and the rest of His grace when we go with their flow and let life open up to us. We have to remember that life on earth should always be viewed "from above" and to do that we have to realize that we are here to learn. Our mistakes and trials are learning opportunities. We are spiritual beings having a physical experience. Instead of letting our mistakes discourage us, we should allow them to energize us.

Be open always to God's perspective.

At our house we have a swale. During intense storms, it fills with water and stays that way for days and even weeks at a time (if there are hurricanes). Initially, this had me concerned. I called the town and was getting agitated when they didn't come out and correct it.

God had another plan.

My son loves fish and frogs. That summer the storms kept water in the swale most of the summer, and hundreds of tadpoles thrived in it — turning into frogs. During one storm a canal backed up and put small fish in it! Every day for several months my son was able to go out and watch the animals in their natural environment. Another time, as the weather dried, I was watering a new tree and forgot to turn the water off. Water is expensive where we live and it ran for hours!

When I stepped back and took a second look I realized the water had drained off the lawn and replenished that swale, saving the lives of the animals!

On another occasion, I wanted to take my family to an alligator park, but the others didn't feel up to it, just my son. Instead we took a ride and ended up renting a small boat for a trip up a creek. Within a few minutes we saw the awesome sight of an alligator my own size there in the wild (much more awesome than a gator park), and then three smaller ones! On the second visit there were eight. On the third there were forty.

"Let go and let God" is the expression, and it's not just a cliche: Just about every day we're faced with a choice between doing things the way we think is best and doing things that flow with the Holy Spirit. When you have that choice, go with the Spirit. God wants us to be thinking, rational persons, but He also wants us to be faithful, fearless, and release things to Him. Too often we set our minds on a plan and attempt to adhere to it so rigidly that we can't hear His small voice within us.

God wants us to approach matters in a freer, more open, and certainly more trustful manner — which means letting Him put things together. Time and again I've seen where I'll have a rigid schedule during a trip or other endeavor — a master plan of how the day should be approached, with detailed plans that I have agonized over. On the other hand, when something unexpected comes up — and I'm open to it — it often leads to remarkable results.

The Lord opens up when we open to Him, and this is a lesson that can save us both time and tremendous internal wrangling. Much of our anxiety is caused by trying to hash out everything ourselves, with our own rigid intellects, instead of asking God to do it for us. By just releasing a plan or schedule, by dismissing rigid control, by stepping back, we invite the miraculous. Despite His enormity, all God needs is a little opening!

Make room for God and look for His Mind more than your own. Let Him flow like the Mississippi. And "pray big." *Don't let the expectations of the world,* of the "logical," limit you. Praying big means praying with openness.

It's only natural to want certain things and to find ourselves striving for them. But it's a mistake. We become unbalanced. We are at constant war with the flesh, and when we lust after something, even something that seems good, this is enough to cause a block. Often the Lord holds back because we want something too much.

Our eyes are supposed to be on Heaven, on the Light at the end of the tunnel (that we can't want too much), and when we turn that focus to something else — something mundane, and especially something selfish — we exhaust our grace.

Forcing an issue can burn a hole in what we are seeking. It can break it. There are times that in His mercy, God grants that we can have something we have overly sought (just as we occasionally give in to a child), but usually He puts up roadblocks, especially if something is not in our best interests. If you think back on your life (the career you may have wanted as a teenager, the girlfriends or boyfriends you would have died to have had, the material possessions you so craved), you'll find that having your way would have been to your profound long-term detriment. As the saying goes, God's greatest grace is in unanswered prayers.

Think back. Go through life and project what would have happened if you had realized some of your fondest desires!

When we die, we will see everything that happened on earth with the clarity of new eyes.

The senseless will make sense. We'll see that *God changes our plans for the better.* He is perfect and knows perfectly well what is best for us. We won't see that whole picture until we are on the "other side" and we may go through life holding onto an old desire. But when we do see the big picture, we'll thank God for not answering many of our most passionate requests. We'll see how prayers that He didn't answer were not answered precisely because of His love. We'll also find that many were not answered because we were violating a spiritual law. Many requests are built on inordinate desire or lust. When we're in Heaven we'll see the many gifts that were hidden in our "misfortunes."

Do you have everything laid out? Are you too set in your ways? Have you decided that you know everything you need to know about what you need?

When you're rigid, you create a shell and grace bounces off of it.

Think of how many ways you may be restricting yourself by being too stiff.

Sometimes this is the sole reason for unanswered prayers:

God wants you to stop yearning so earnestly and to let things unfold in His timing. What you desire may be in His plan for you, but He may be waiting for you to stop obsessing over it.

Nothing inhibits the miraculous more than trying to entirely control a situation.

The solution, after sufficient prayer, is to let go and put it into God's Hands. That's easier said than done, but when we step back and let God direct our lives – when we stop striving, in the belief that we must be in control — it's miraculous how life can unfold and how peaceful it becomes.

Do not seek what others have. God gives everyone equal gifts. Often we look around and think everyone has more gifts, more "talent," more possessions, than we do, but in fact if we have the simple gift of making someone happy, if we can love with all our hearts, if we have patience, we have the greatest gifts of all. While the person who is a famous actor or writer or a leader seems to have it all, seems to be loaded with gifts, the opposite may be true. You may have much more. You may be a receptionist, gifted with the ability to smile. Do we realize how important that is? A "simple" smile may turn around a person's entire day — and lead to a chain reaction. To make someone happy is a great gift and more than the vast majority of famous "gifted" people can claim. Are you good at taking care of kids? This is extremely important to God. He likes nothing more. Do you have the gift of housework (done without complaint)?

God loves the hidden and simple and if he has kept you that way, this too is a gift. A balanced person is a tranquil person and tranquility is a miracle.

Life on earth is a constant struggle to find our equilibrium.

On our way to that balance, God sends us favors as indications. Most are small. They add up. There are also the little admonishments. Some are not so little. Mostly we are punished by the lack of His Presence. When we abuse anything God has given to us, we lose our equilibrium and we become stuck in a life that is a hum-drum litany of the non-miraculous.

This is why we find so many escaping to TV: there is no electricity in their own lives. When we need anything that is artificial, we are looking for fulfillment in the wrong places. Think of all the time spent in front of a computer or the television that could have been spent in prayer. If just a quarter of that time had been devoted to communicating with God, amazing things would have occurred. When we pray, the Holy Spirit naturally begins to bring us into balance and our lives become structured in a way that makes them receptive to miracles. The act of being positive initiates this process while the negative turns miracles away. It expects something bad, and often draws it (unless it is necessary warning, as Jesus warned in *Matthew* 24). Nothing could be more counter-productive. To be negative is to lack constructive features. Worse yet, negativity is usually a lie. God is the God of light and has good things – painful things at times, yes, trying things, but in the end good things — waiting for us, when we don't turn negative and (through pride) resist them. What a tragedy it is to see someone respond to a difficult situation with negative feelings that only make the problem worse and negate the grace that would otherwise be attached to the suffering!

Chapter 43

Don't limit the blessings God has in store for you

Thus says the LORD: "If you remove from your midst oppression, false accusation and malicious speech; If you bestow your bread on the hungry and satisfy the afflicted; Then light shall rise for you in the darkness, and the gloom shall become for you like midday; Then the LORD will guide you always and give you plenty even on the parched land. He will renew your strength, and you shall be like a watered garden, like a spring whose water never fails" (*Isaiah* 58:9-14).

Go with the flow. Let life open up to you. To repeat: don't force things.

We should always wait on the Lord, and we should always follow His timetable.

Frustrated? In want of something that just isn't happening? Can't figure out why prayers aren't answered? There's only one solution: Let go of whatever it is you are yearning for and send it into God's Hands. Trust beyond surrender. Put your mind on other matters. Anxiety inhibits grace and can be caused by the spirit of fear. This fear can come in many ways. It can be the product of repeated action on our part, or it can be a familial trait. We inherit spiritual baggage just as we inherit anything else, and it's a mixture of good and bad. There are spirits of gluttony, lust, sloth, infirmity, despair, greed, rebellion, impurity, and addiction. We see how divorce runs in certain families. Usually, it's a combination of factors. Spirits magnify our weaknesses. If we are prone to nervousness, a spirit of anxiety or even paranoia may develop within us, inhibiting happiness. A disposition toward procrastination may turn into a spirit of sloth; a dabbling with the occult, or a yearning for control, can turn into the spirit of dominance (or even witchcraft). This all bears repeating.

As it says in *Ephesians* (6:16), faith should be held up as a shield against the fiery darts of the evil one, which are then extinguished.

One of the great needs in the modern Church is a return to the practice of deliverance. Around the world, thousands suffer from demonic problems that are ignored, misdiagnosed, or discarded as "superstitious."

It is not superstition. Our thoughts manifest in reality. When those who have near-death experiences return, they express astonishment at how when the Lord reviewed their lives, He considered every single act they did, word they spoke, and thought they had. He took them gently but with honesty through every single event in their lives and let them feel exactly how they made others feel (good or bad). They saw themselves in an entirely new perspective – including from the perspective of those with whom they had interacted.

"The words we are pronouncing say much about ourselves," noted a Croatian priest named Father Ljubo Kurtovi. "A word can wound and heal, it can kill and bring back to life. This is why it is important to overcome what is bad and evil within us with what is good, pure, and blessed. Whatever is blessed brings blessing. Bless a thing and it will bless you! Curse it and it will curse you! Whatever you judge in your life will come back to you and hurt you. If you bless a situation, it has no more strength to hurt you and, even if for a time it causes you trouble, little by little this trouble will disappear, and the blessing coming from a pure heart will become a blessing for others. When you bless, you become ready to receive blessing. Blessing is the strength and the light for our paths. Through the blessing, light and peace enter into us. As soon as someone starts to bless instead of curse, wishing good to others instead of cursing them, he becomes healthy, happy, and saved from the hands of the enemy."

Begin a pattern of praying for every person you have encountered in your life, right from the time you were born, even passing strangers. This clears negativity you or they may have set in motion and opens the door for blessings. *Blessings reverse the curse* while sending a harmful thought not only curses the other person but the person who sent it.

It is true that what goes around comes around. We receive what we have given. It is especially true of love. The other shield is meekness. "If you are humble," said Mother Teresa, "nothing will touch you."

Repeat to yourself frequently, "I will be meek today."

Has someone said something negative? Shake it off. Dust it from your shoes. The dispelling of negativity is the preparation for wonders. Learn this as a first step. While there are times when we are in need of correction, and in humility should accept it, that's different than accepting negativity. Negativity is Satan's way of binding us to discouragement, and at its first appearance, we must take time to reject it and firmly root it out. The more we do that (the more we learn to brush off evil), the easier it becomes and the cleaner we are. Correction can hurt, but handled well, it always causes improvements, even through disasters, which arrive to simplify us and will continue to do so.

"Just trust in my Son Jesus."

Keep your eyes on the God of miracles.

He loves you more than you love yourself and sees the potential you have to be with Him in eternity. He knows that beneath the exterior, under the skin of the earthly body — and often deep under the burdens of life — is a being of tremendous beauty waiting to burst out of the cocoon and move skyward with the eyes of love. With those eyes we elevate our vision above turmoil and beyond any problem — to see the best of outcomes. When we elevate our eyes, when we look above those who harass us, when we see beyond trials on earth, we are seeing into the miraculous.

No matter how "severe," we're on the road of glory. It's what Christ saw on the Cross. It's the Heaven He had in mind, even as He was crucified.

Projecting love to those who may not wish you the best can overcome a stubborn problem and is how futile prayers are answered. "God has created us to love and to be loved, and this is the beginning of prayer — to know that He loves me, to know that I have been created for greater things," said Mother Teresa.

The sky is the limit when we have faith and when we go to God as a child, shedding our worldliness. To be a child is to lose the crustiness we have built around us.

Too often, we pray as if we're confined in a closet. While that's a good place to go for privacy, we're not supposed to limit ourselves, and most often we do. We believe only to a *point*. We set limits. We restrain the blessings God has in store for us!

We need to open up. We need to think big. When we're working for Jesus He will bless and help us accomplish the impossible. He'll expand our territory — often in a way that's miraculous.

There is no use allowing yourself to be oppressed by life. There is the need to rise above it. When we feel down, when we have problems, we need to pray as if we *know* we will be heard. Don't be afraid to ask, nor to ask beyond what you normally expect (*John* 16:24).

God loves our requests. They honor Him. He loves to bless. But we have to ask through a clear channel – one devoid of fear — and all of us should do that every day: ask for better and bigger blessings and better and bigger ways of serving and living His glory here and forever!

Clear your spirit, especially of fear. If the Bible says that perfect love casts away fear, how much love do we have if we are full of fear? If you're afraid, step up your prayer. Pray from the heart. Fast and pray a lot longer. It's then that the Spirit comes, and nothing can be frightening when we have the Holy Spirit?

Chapter 44

The secret formula is a race to His embrace

And persevere.

Often we miss out on a miracle because we gave up or simply didn't pray enough.

Once I spotted a severe thunderstorm coming. It had not been predicted by the weatherman, yet it looked very intense, the most swiftly-moving, blackest clouds I'd ever seen. It was a localized storm, heading directly our way, and it was hurling tremendous bolts of lightning.

Immediately I asked God to keep the lightning off our property and it was a very specific request: that it not hit our house. Quickly, I made the Sign of the Cross to "cover" our lot.

The storm struck and lightning hit, all right – missing our house, hitting just feet from our back property line.

That was an answer to a prayer – and a specific answer at that. It missed our yard! But the story doesn't end there. There was a surge of electricity that swept underground, carrying into the power, cable, and telephone lines, which caused problems in our home.

Our burglar alarm had to be replaced. Two outlets were burned out. A computer was damaged.

And in my mind the reason was simple: I had not persevered. I had not prayed long or thoroughly enough. I had uttered the quick prayer of protection over our property and that had worked, but I had not prayed to protect us from any surge, had not prayed to protect specific items like our computers, alarm system, and other equipment, and had not prayed for the neighborhood in general.

There was a miracle in how the storm had missed us but the miracle could have been bigger. With more prayer, we would not have lost any equipment.

Complete prayer brings larger results.

Why do storms serve as such a good example?

It was during a storm that Jesus admonished His disciples to step out of the boat and into the realm of miracles.

So too must we step out of the boat. With faith anything can happen, on any scale, and the accounts come to me (at our website, www.spiritdaily.com) on a daily basis. I know a woman who had severely broken her leg and went to Medjugorje ("stepped out of the boat") and encountered a mysterious stranger and soon after startled the doctors when her bone grew back. "You've been healed!" screeched a medical assistant, holding her x-rays. "You've been healed!"

The Lord can appear at any time, in any situation. There is never reason not to persevere. There is not a single miracle that you do not have the potential to tap into. We have seen accounts – right unto death – of how perseverance pays off. We have seen mountains moved. Usually, they are smaller mountains, bumps in our lives, that we need help over. When we have resistance, we have to remember that there are spiritual forces unique even to certain areas, forces that can intermingle with our own vulnerable spirits. These need to be cleansed.

Life on earth is a constant invisible transaction. Our victories often seem like "minor" victories, but they are no less miraculous. The money that came when you needed it? That lonely child of yours who suddenly has a buddy?

"Small" victories, but perhaps not really all that small.

We see such miracles every day and refer to them as answered prayers. It's the way that the God of miracles coordinates our lives when we are in tune with Him and are selfless. I once received a Christmas card that listed the various ways of "dying to self." It was eye-opening. It described dying to self as:

- "when you are forgotten or neglected and you don't hurt with the insult, but your heart is happy — that is dying to self

- "when your advice is disregarded, your opinions ridiculed, and you refuse to let anger rise in your heart, and take it all in patient, loving silence — that is dying to self

- "when you lovingly and patiently bear disorder, irregularity, tardiness, and annoyance... and endure it as Jesus endured it — that is dying to self

- "when you never care to refer to yourself in conversation or record your own good works, or itch for praise after an accomplishment, when you can truly love to be unknown... that is dying to self

- "when you can see your brother or sister prosper and can honestly rejoice with him, and feel no envy even though your needs are greater — that is dying to self

- "when you are content with any food, any offering, any raiment, any climate, or any society — that is dying to self

- "when you can take correction, when you can humbly submit inwardly as well as outwardly, with no rebellion or resentment rising up within your heart — that is dying to self."

Slowly but surely, we must reorient our lives; it takes patience. Life on earth is a constant struggle to balance our moods, diligent in our work, steadfast in our prayer, and full of constant love, which is the true power of the universe and what will propel us upward.

Nothing is tragic when it assists our march to Heaven.

You'll see why I say that in a minute.

We are here to purify our intentions, to purge our spirits of evil, and when we do that we have nothing to fear. To purify an intention is to dramatically change the way we view everything we do, and even everything we think, so that all is oriented toward service to God.

We don't have to be clerics to do it. We need only to orient our actions with God as the first thought. Step back and always let Him be the first thing on your mind.

The questions we must always ask:

What does He need from me? How can I best glorify Him in the tasks I have been given? How can I use my station in life to further His cause, and all of His creation?

Perhaps we are created imperfect because in rectifying those imperfections we come to a more profound love of God. Is that the purpose? When we think of imperfections like hatred and anger and gossip and pride, these fall away only as our love for Him grows. Our lives should be a "race to His embrace."

Most of us are on distorted missions that revolve around ourselves and that serve as a hindrance to the supernatural. The first thing we should consider in everything we do is not how it will affect *us*, how it will make *us* feel, but instead how it will make God feel. Usually, and tragically, it's the opposite. *We* have to do this. *We* have to do that. *We* desire. *We* want. Our missions have been distorted into self-seeking instead of God-seeking, which is at the root of many of our problems and the reason we so often fall. We build a house for ourselves. We buy a car because *we* like the car. We work to receive money that tends to our own needs, which too often means our egos.

There is nothing wrong with tending to legitimate needs and enjoying *what* He provides *but God has to be at the center of it.* Every waking moment we have to view our lives as a mission for Him. Everything should be with God in mind. How do we do that if we're not in a spiritual line of work and our work has nothing to do with religion? We *make* what we do a mission. We see ourselves as clandestine God-agents. We minister through what we say or pray whether we are doctors, lawyers, insurance agents, trash collectors, or mechanics. All afford an opportunity to pray for others. This doesn't mean we have to walk around the office handing out Bible tracts, nor that we have to wear sandwich boards. A small act of kindness – doing the laundry when it isn't our chore, washing an older person's car, touching someone who needs to be touched, offering pain and sacrifice and even the tedium of work to God – is pleasing to Him. They go into a bank. And every single one of us has them to offer. In our work itself, there is almost always an aspect of what we do to further His cause. *Every vocation, save for obviously notorious ones, has a Godly component.* If nothing else, we can minister to those around us. We can pray. Praying for all those around us (at the bank, in an insurance office, at the supermarket) is an excellent mission. When we seek the miraculous life only for ourselves, it becomes a mirror of the culture around us. Like a mirror, it will show a false picture (all mirrors show things in reverse); it will also crack; it is only true on the surface.

A safe life is a deep life lived for God. When we approach each day from the perspective of His mission instead of our own, we are on the way to opening doors we didn't even know existed, doors behind which, as I have emphasized, are graces in store for us. The apparition seen by that Marine in Viet Nam matched one depicted in the famous Catholic apparition known as the "Miraculous Medal" – during which the Blessed Mother, appearing to a nun who would later become a saint, appeared with rings on her fingers, each set with gems that radiated. It was explained to the nun that the rays from the gems were the symbols of graces that came from Christ and that Mary, as His assistant, shed upon those who asked for them. *"The gems from which rays do not fall,"* she said, *"are the graces for which souls forget to ask."*

We need to stop and think about what we may be missing! Those gems come when we are seeking His embrace and have taken the time to humbly ask for them.

Once received, such graces are enhanced every time we are diligent, overcome a bad habit, confess a sin (making a real effort not to repeat it), or turn away from what tempts us. God blesses us to encourage us in good and withdraws blessings to indicate when we are in error. Graces are enhanced every time we turn the other cheek. I have seen a number of cases where what seemed like a disaster caused by the evil of another was simply ignored and followed by graces that greatly exceeded what the evil took away. *Every temptation is a gift* because it is the chance to be more like Jesus.

Be real with yourself and do not bind yourself to material things but to God. And do not forget that your life is transitory like a flower.

Do not fear but see it at the root of other negative emotions. Fear is often the reason we dislike others, limit what we do, and isolate ourselves.

The more we overcome negative emotional reactions, the more we begin to feel peace, happiness, and freedom.

There is what is called a stream of life that flows from God and in Scripture it is called the "living waters." It's crystalline and like regular water, but is actually sparkling grace. It is impeded only when we throw rocks into it.

Those rocks are our tendencies to selfishness, which cause the "water" to divert around us.

When water is forced around a rock, it tends to get rough. If there are too many rocks, they plug the stream like a dam.

Our goal in life, our path to the miraculous, and to Heaven, is to remove whatever boulders may be in the stream of life that has been designated for us. In that way do we quicken the flow, letting the stream come with full fruition. That occurs through the purity of our intentions.

From there, we have to let ourselves flow with it. That means releasing many of our tensions, timetables, troubles, anxieties, and routines to God, knowing that He is there when we need Him. He monitors events in our lives much more closely than we ourselves could ever hope to monitor them and while He may take His time, He is never late.

Give everything to God and don't worry. Jesus said that the "anxiety of the world" makes us "unfruitful." When we worry it's a little stone that collects on top of other "worry stones." Eventually, there will be a block; fear is like a boulder.

To attract the stream of life, we must shake off fear and become as pure as the heavenly flow. The worst enemy you have may be on your wrist. When we are slaves to time, we are slaves to the flow of what man has created, instead of the flow of God, Who is timeless.

"All for God and all for others" is the slogan of the wonderworker.

If you seek God and work for Him in everything, without pause, the result will be miraculous.

When we have failure, we have to investigate the reasons behind it. It could just be a test, or as I just said, God's way of nudging us from something that really isn't good for us. It could also be the result of something wrong that we have done (or are still doing), and for which we must atone. *Going back through our lives,* we should review every major event, good and bad, and ask ourselves what we took from it. Did we learn from it? Did we improve? Are we focusing our prayers on getting over the hurdle the next time it comes? Remember that trials come in ways that are mostly unexpected – defeated only when prayer has been our preparation.

At other times, we should realize the need for trials. Tests afford an opportunity to step closer to Heaven. God is good and allows us to do some of our purgatory here on earth. We follow Jesus and His cross. When we realize that, there is no longer the room for bitterness. I remember a conversation I had with the former Marine who described the passing of his wife from cancer and how it brought him closer to God. The nurturing of her during that difficult death showed him spiritual truths that otherwise would not have been shown. His response of joy, even in this great "tragedy," filled him with grace: to this day, many claim that his prayers have healed or converted them. Her death was a gift to the both of them! He later began a ministry of hand-fashioning gorgeous rosaries and shedding tears of joy while he made them.

These tears he rubs into the beads as sort of an anointing.

All of us should likewise reflect on our lives and meditate on why certain unfortunate things may have occurred and what we can learn and produce from them.

God gave us free will. We are like sparks from the fire of His love and the test of life is whether we will return to Him or continue on as sparks into darkness. When we make choices for love, we are coming back to His Light.

The most "unmiraculous" thing we can do is distance ourselves from Him through disbelief, indifference, or anger. Everything is set in our paths for a reason and the longer we walk with God, the more we recognize the truth that there are no accidents. All events have some kind of purpose; only God fully understands what that purpose is. But we can say this: often, He allows chaos to erupt around us. He does that because He needs to *stir* in order to cook. He wants to rearrange things. Our task is to submit. When we die, God will not judge on whether we met every single challenge in an absolutely perfect way but rather by how we made the attempt. What He wants is acknowledgement of Him in all circumstances.

When there is suffering or sorrow it usually opens us to a new perspective. This should be held in high value: for when we have a new perspective, we have an opportunity to cleanse or expel another part of our selves. It is in trial that we view our failings with an opportunity to transform them.

"Well done," the Lord will say when we have tried with all our hearts in every event (however mixed the results). Doing what we least want to do and offering it to Him is a powerful way of remaining in contact.

"What have you learned?" was the first thing that Jesus asked one woman who had a near-death experience.

Let us ask ourselves that each day.

We are here to learn, and we can learn from anything or anybody, especially those who are difficult to love, or even hostile. Look at everything and everyone for what they are: opportunities to advance. We will see the repeat of certain trials until we learn how to deal with them, and so perhaps "practice" is a better word than "test." God gives us a lot of practice! In life we test each other and pass the tests by realizing them for the tests that they are.

This awareness comes from remaining in touch with God and releasing all to Him. The keys to peace are:

- Learning to do the best we can and then saying, "God will tend to it; it doesn't matter." Leave the consequences to Him.

- Learning to say, "I surrender all to God; I no longer need to control or be ambitious as the world knows ambition."

- Learning to say: "I will be steadfast but will not rush. I know that God ripens His fruit slowly." (Remember again that the anxiety of the world makes us unfruitful.)

- Learning to say, "I will put love where there is the first sign of negativity. I will see beyond a person to the spirit. I will judge no one!"

- Repeating always, "I will confess." And making sure that there is regular Confession.

- Saying in all tribulation: "I will pour out my heart to God."

- And expressing to Him that "I want to help others instead of myself."

This means flowing in tune with God, letting go of material obsessions, and praying with faith no matter what happens — knowing "unanswered" prayers are placed in that "bank" for a future surprise. Did you know that God loves to surprise you?

I've spoken to so many in ministry who have seen funds materialize miraculously. In Nebraska are nuns who have needed something like curtains or carpeting and have seen a check arrive for the exact amount they needed, down to the dollar. God wants us to know He is there. There is even a novena to Our Lady of Surprises, and after writing about it one day, my wife and I were shocked by the behavior of our children: normally not the neatest (like any kids their age), suddenly, that same afternoon, they were scurrying about the house cleaning everything in sight – not just their own rooms, but the living room, kitchen, dining room, bathrooms, and family room, the entire house, and quite professionally. They were only eight and nine but spent hours – out of the blue – doing this for no apparent reason!

What a surprise that was. What surprises He has for you. God has both a sense of humor and blessings for everyone, blessings waiting to be claimed, whether they are corporal blessings (a new job, a spouse, a solution to a problem) or spiritual blessings. The grace could be suffering. It could be the grace of patience. It could be more faith. Grace flows every time we meet a challenge and tap more deeply into the stream of life.

We tap into it through practices like reading the Bible (fifteen minutes a day can work wonders) or partaking of Communion. This is important. We must take our prayer to the Eucharist. Many are the requests that are granted from prayers raised while the priest elevates the Host. Demons are tossed out when the Precious Blood is held high and as we partake of it.

That sacrament, when coupled with forgiveness, brings tremendous healing. But first ask God to reveal any sins you need to confess or anything you need to forgive — then watch the blessings flow! The holy practices we have been taught – in whatever aspect of the Church – have real benefit. During the Eucharist, the stream is channeled through the Host in the same way that light streams from the sun. Perhaps this is why so many see "sun miracles" with a Host in front of it.

From such practices come blessings you don't even know are there: happiness, security, and contentment are among them. I remember an unforgettable moment while visiting Assisi, Italy, near the tomb of the great

St. Francis. Walking up a road through an olive orchard after praying at a small chapel, I reached for a green olive and without thinking bit into it. I had no idea that it wasn't ripe, and my taste buds immediately were overwhelmed by the most bitter taste I'd ever encountered – such that I couldn't wait to find a water fountain. I needed to wash the taste away! Quickly I made my way to the main basilica, my goal a water fountain, but after just a minute or two, there was a phenomenal transformation in my mouth. The bitterness left and in its place was a taste so sweet that there is nothing I can cite in comparison.

I don't know how that happened. Was it a trick of my taste buds? I know only that a bitter moment had turned into one that was utterly delectable – as bitter moments do for us all when we are walking in the right place, in the right direction, and in the right circumstances. The Lord surprises with His unfailing generosity.

He may *well* be ready to give you what you have sought for so long but may be waiting for you to see His goodness in every aspect of life and to completely turn over your life to Him.

Know that there are blessings around the corner. Have faith! That potent combination will loose many gifts and lift you in a way that will exceed your best Christmas. *See every problem as an opportunity,* for thankfulness in all situations unlocks grace. When that is kept in mind, it brings the realization that there is never the need for desperation.

What a realization that is! I have heard so many accounts of miracles, miracles that often tax even the greatest credulity. One healer I cited has detailed the healing of a man who had a lung removed and a rib along with it. After the healer prayed over him, the rib suddenly appeared on x-rays.

It is mindful of a remarkably well-documented case in San Giovanni Rotundo, Italy, in which the missing eye of a construction worker was said to have rematerialized after St. Padre Pio prayed for him. When the bandage was taken off, there was the eye despite detailed medical descriptions of how it had been obliterated in a blasting accident.

Doctors had *seen* the empty socket.

Can we believe such accounts? We are not to become overly credulous. At the same time, think back to what Christ said about moving mountains.

Miracles are all around, if we would only notice. Think of birth. What could be more miraculous than one unique and fully formed person coming from another? No purely physical process can account for it and all day every day, God incorporates the natural with the supernatural. Isaac Newton came to appreciate the spiritual side of life when he "clearly saw God as an essential part of nature, the 'first cause' on which everything else depended." Meanwhile, Saint Albert the Great wrote brilliantly on how without God we are nothingness surrounded by nothingness — that we must realize He made us, preserves us, causes us to react, enlivens us, emboldens us, gives us the very energy to move, and in the end draws us closer to Him, if we go along with it.

The more we appreciate the interchange between the physical and spiritual, the more we flow in the stream of life, which means gaining momentum toward larger miracles. Building faith means watching little prayers build into bigger ones.

How good is God! How miraculous! That He would even create us! When we see the constant miracles of life, we begin to view everything from a spiritual perspective.

All day, every day, through the mind, our spirits interact with the world around us. It is from the spirit that the directive goes to the mind and is then translated to the brain, which signals the neurons in the body.

We are above the physical and when we view life in such a way, we begin to develop mastery over it.

As Jesus showed when He cursed a fig tree, we react with our physical surroundings. If we wish something well, it flourishes, while negativity is like a curse that darkens the spiritual (and then the physical) landscape. What is a bolt of lightning but a brief, large current of negative charge, and what is a hurricane but a barometer that is headed downward?

Think of it again as plus and minus. Plus gives. Plus has energy. Negative takes. Negative is hollow. Positive is full. Negative says "no" – including to serving God. The positive says yes.

Yes to God, yes to faithfulness, yes to love, yes to happiness.

From the standpoint of God, Who sees what we cannot, the greatest earthly "tragedy" is just a passing bad moment. The key to gaining Heaven is to live every moment in the way we would want to be judged. The key is to live each moment as if it is our last. When we have eternity on our minds, we lose the negative. Our hearts are filled with gladness, which is a miracle, a gift like every gift that flows from the Holy Spirit. It is available to everyone and joins the important component of hope, which means to look at all matters from a positive aspect: not a Pollyanna aspect, where we try to make it seem like even something truly bad is good, but rather a knowing that there is a light at the end of tunnel – literally.

For this is the final miracle: our own "resurrection."

We too rise from the "dead," not as a full corporal body, like Jesus, but with full consciousness. I've received testimonies and read hundreds of those accounts in which a person clinically died and glimpsed the other side, confirming those statements. While science would like us to believe that this is mere wishful thinking – or an anoxic (oxygen-depriving) reaction in the brain – the scenes that unfold are far too consistent and cohesive to be fragments of the subconscious.

They are not "dreams." They hold together as actual events – even more so. Those who have near-death brushes say they felt more aware and alive than they ever had, that they were aware every moment, keenly aware, right to the parting of their spirits.

When we die, at the moment that bodily functions come to a halt, the spiritual force will rise and head like a globe of light (if we recall St. Hildegarde) for another dimension.

When I mentioned "tunnel," it's because so many who have near-death experiences describe that tunnel-like passage that transported them through space and time to a Light they widely describe as Jesus. He is the mediator. He is the maestro of wonders!

And would you believe that with Him there is no fear *even in death,* even in tragedy? Many are those who have headed into the realm of Heaven before they came back and they say the same thing: that Jesus was there and there was nothing whatsoever to fear. Most found it to be the most enjoyable experience of their lives. Most did not want to return. In the spiritual state, they inform us, one is more aware than ever. Our seeing and hearing and thinking are clearer than when we are on earth. Perception widens. We see objects from all angles, instead of from one side. There are the colors that go far beyond the three primary ones (dozens of new "primaries") and music beyond earthly music and the peace of now realizing that we are spiritual beings, capable of true wonders, beings who live forever.

This goes to Scripture, where Paul talked about "a man in Christ" who "fourteen years ago — whether in the body I do not know, or out of the body I do not know, God knows — such a man was caught up to the third heaven."

Millions around the world report similar experiences.

And their testimony is consistent right down to details of the light they saw, the way they left their bodies, and other sensations. "It was a big surprise to me to have this sense of something different than the body — a consciousness different than the body — and to be in this wonderfully healing, peaceful, nurturing place," noted a cell biologist who died when a falling window hit her.

Even those who died in what appeared to those watching as painful, "tragic" deaths describe death as pleasant. In fact, though they come back with a greater appreciation for life (and their missions), they never fear death again. To a man, they describe the feeling of Heaven as returning to a true origin. If there was a collective way of relating how they felt, it would be: *This is my real home! I'm home! I'm finally home!* They look forward to the time when God calls them back.

They were embraced with a love that we on earth cannot comprehend.

There is no greater lesson than that death is not to be feared when we have the assistance of Christ (it loses its "sting") and there is no greater miracle than eternity.

"I began to experience the most wonderful feelings," said one person. "I couldn't feel a thing in the world except peace, comfort, ease – just quietness. I felt that all my troubles were gone, and I thought to myself, 'Well, how quiet and peaceful, and I don't hurt at all.'"

"I had the feeling that I was moving through a deep, very dark valley," said another. "The darkness was so deep and impenetrable that I could see absolutely nothing but this was the most wonderful, worry-free experience you can imagine."

If there is dark, it is only a passage. The most common description is the Light.

God is love. Love is light. Light is life. God is the Light of life that loves. What heals is love; what kills is judgment. The Light itself is only love. Of all the teachings, the greatest is love. It is accompanied by joy, which is the truest sign that we are living right. Joy in all, joy in Jesus.

"Whenever a person turns to the Lord the veil is removed," says *2 Corinthians* 3:15. "Now the Lord is the Spirit and where the Spirit of the Lord is, there is freedom. All of us, gazing with unveiled face on the glory of the Lord, are being transformed into the same image from glory to glory, as from the Lord Who is the Spirit."

As it continues:

"For God Who said, Let light shine out of darkness, has shone in our hearts to bring to light the knowledge of the glory of God on the face of

Jesus Christ."

It is through Jesus that we find eternity. Christ told us that "I am the resurrection and the life. If anyone believes in Me, even though he dies, he will live. And whoever lives and believes in Me will never die" (*John* 11:25-26).

In many ways, the greatest miracle of life is the miracle of death.

We live forever! When we die, there is no "sleep." There is no fade to black. We die in full consciousness.

"While in the tunnel, I experienced a total change when touched by the Light," testified an Australian woman. "When this overwhelming unconditional love flowed over me, and through me, every atom of my soul was bathed and altered in its light. All my scars, and bad memories, vanished instantly. None of it mattered except this love I was receiving. None of the bad times seemed real at that point. They were only learning experiences, and I could feel them flowing away, all the pain gone; just this wonderful timeless moment, where I was totally accepted for who I was, and where I had come from."

"Suddenly, an enormous explosion erupted beneath me, an explosion of light rolling out to the farthest limits of my vision," said another woman. "I was in the center of the Light. It blew away everything, including the fog. It reached the ends of the universe, which I could see, and doubled back on itself in endless layers. I was watching eternity unfold. The Light was brighter than hundreds of suns, but it did not hurt my eyes. I had never seen anything as luminous or as golden as this Light, and I immediately understood it was entirely composed of love, all directed at me. This wonderful, vibrant love was very personal, as you might describe secular love, but also sacred. Though I had never seen God, I recognized this light as the Light of God. But even the word God seemed too small to describe the magnificence of that Presence. I was with my Creator, in holy communication with that Presence. The Light was directed at me and through me; it surrounded me and pierced me. It existed just for me. The Light gave me knowledge, though I heard no words. We did not communicate in English or in any other language. This was discourse clearer and easier than the clumsy medium of language. It was something like understanding math or music -- nonverbal knowledge, but knowledge no less profound. I was learning the answers to the eternal questions of life — questions so old we laugh them off as clichés."

What is life? Why is there the battle between good and evil? These were some of the questions those who died have presented to Christ, and it gets back to that "spark": He is the Light that we as sparks came from. In that light, one was shown that we are players in a "courtroom" drama in which Satan is trying to prove to God that mankind is only in it for himself, that we love God only for what we can get out of Him. God has faith in us and believes the opposite: that despite afflictions and temptations, despite the hardships of life, we will return to Him. Do we love God for Himself or for what we can get out of Him? This in the end is the most important of all questions. "We are in the process of a big court case, because this question has to be solved by mankind," she said. "That's why the choices we make, for love or for darkness, are very, very important choices. We're not the ones on trial so much as making the evidence, that we can not do this ourselves. It's basically that the devil wants us in confusion and darkness. Mankind is in the middle of it. There is a watching and a gathering of evidence. Will we continue on as sparks to darkness or come back to God and the Light? When we make choices for love, we are coming closer back to Him."

And in the Light of eternity, even our largest problems are minor. As one policeman from Omaha told me, "When I was on the other side I realized there are no big deals here on earth."

That is: what we think is so important here is just a moment in time.

We are never without hope. Each one of us is God's favorite. We are never alone. "I have seen many, many patients pass away and it has totally taken away my fear of dying," psychotherapist Dr. Verushka Biddle, who works with the seriously ill, told me. "I observe such a wonderful peace. What they see at that moment must be so incredible that I think death is by far the most beautiful experience that we ever have."

Dr. Biddle went on to say that this includes accidents — that people with serious injuries also gain that painlessness (and peace) at the moment of death.

They are seeing something we can't. They see the Light. She says she has seen indications that saints like Padre Pio are present. And the psychotherapist says it's common for those dying to slip into a different sort of consciousness two or three days before their expiration and encounter deceased loved ones who have come to help them with the transition.

Is this not miraculous? We are all reunited with loved ones. Everyone knows everyone and will see almost everyone forever. Hope is a miracle, and hope springs eternal because it is from the eternal. In the end, objects mean nothing; it is only people who count. And once more, it gets back to love, which is the energy of God Himself. God is love. With Him, we are never alone. We see Him in the birds that fly. We see Him in the colorful contours of a butterfly. We see Him in a child's waking eyes. And we connect with Him through the positive. That means we say "yes," yes to God, yes to faith, yes to happiness. When we do that, life is a carnival of miracles.

Find your purpose in life. Live it to its fullest. Do not be a slave to time. Appreciate things for what they are – not for what they can give you. Do not allow yourself to be dominated by the thoughts or expectations of others. Remember, you are not your body. Your very existence is a miracle. Fear not – even pain and certainly not death.

There is joy where there was despair. We are never without hope. We are never alone. The purpose of the miraculous is to show us that God exists.

And knowing that, we never fear again.

• • •

Notes

The report on George Bamba is from the *Pacific Daily News,* July 5, 2005. The account of the man in Dayton who received the call is from a video, *Miracles Are Real.* The New York woman whose son survived being run over by an SUV was in the March 12, 2005, *New York Post.* One healer quoted is Bob Rice, whose book is *Former Pentecostal Pastor Speaks Our on the Holy Eucharist.* One account of angelic activity came from the writings of angel expert Joan Wester Anderson, whose most well-known work is, *Where Angels Walk.* The account of Jon Stockton comes from the website for the Christian Broadcast Network. The Punta Gorda anecdote on Sacred Heart is from the August 16, 2004, *Washington Post* and the August 15, 2004 *Palm Beach Post.* The headline on Charley and its sharp turn was in the August 16, 2004, online edition of *News Scientist.*

The Rutkoski quotes come from his book, *Miracles and How to Work Them* (Gospa Missions). Aspects of the discussion on the universe are from *Time* Magazine, November 29, 2004. The account about Joy English is from The Associated Press on December 3, 2004. The story about Lin Peng is from *The Times Colonist,* August 20, 2004. The quote from William Simon is from his book *A Time for Reflection.* The story of the California lottery winner was from the Associated Press on December 7, 2004. The *Baton Rouge Advocate* ran the article on Dr. Logarbo on December 12, 2004. The figure of 73 percent of doctors comes from a survey conducted in 2004 of 1,100 physicians by the Louis Finkelstein Institute for Religious and Social Studies of The Jewish Theological Seminary in New York City. Kimberly Clark's quote is from her book, *After the Light.*

The quote in the last chapter on the sparks and the courtroom is from, Tiffany Snow, author of *The Power of Divine: A Healer's Guide.* The quote on angels is from Dr. Howard Storm's *My Descent into Death.* The study on wealthy was reported on Beliefnet.com (a site with which we have a number of spiritual differences). The "pruning" analogy comes from a book, *Secrets of the Vine,* by Bruce Wilkinson. The internet site with the report from Mongolia on those raised from the "dead" is "Dawn's Fax." The quotes from Father DeGrandis come from his little booklet, "Forgiveness and Inner Healing," available at www.spiritdaily.com. The writer I referenced on kindness was Lawrence G. Lovasik in *Kindness.* The account of the World Trade Center angel was in the Journal News, a suburban newspaper north of New York. The angels associated with President Ronald Reagan are mentioned in *Hand of Providence: The Strong and Quiet Faith of Ronald Reagan*, by Mary Beth Brown. The woman quoted on prayer as beams of light is Betty Eadie, whose book *Embraced By the Light* had seminal information but whose views were later influenced by what could be considered Mormonism or the New Age, meaning we have some theological differences. The lessons from the afterlife are from researcher Kenneth Ring, in his book *Lessons from the Light*. For Padre Pio, see *Padre Pio: The True Story*, by C. Bernard Ruffin. Many accounts previously appeared on www.spiritdaily.com.